I MATTER TOO!

Finding Meaning in Your Life at Any Age

Harlan Rector and Edward Mickolus
VOLUME TWO

Cross & Partners
Ponte Vedra, Florida

PRAISE FOR *I MATTER, VOLUME 1*

"*I Matter: Finding Meaning in Your Life at Any Age,* a fascinating collection in a slim volume that will have you eagerly flipping pages and asking for more. These stories are about childhood, teenage years, adulthood, work and career, family and retirement. Some are inspirational, many are a testament to faith, others will make you laugh, a few will bring tears."

—Florida Times-Union

"New book on an important topic. With politics drowning us like a tsunami and screens of all sizes demanding our attention, a collection of memoirs about what really matters reminds us to take time for things that are important if not urgent at the moment."

—Rev. Robert Kyte, retired minister in the United Church of Christ currently serving as Bridge Pastor for the Hancock (NH) Congregational Church

DEDICATION

To everyone who has made, and continues to make,
a difference in our lives.

TABLE OF CONTENTS

Editors' Introduction

In volume I of this series we asked authors to explore how someone made a (positive) difference in their life or how they made a difference in someone's life. We've been heartened by the response to our request, and to the collection overall. We've asked individuals from all walks of life—a movie producer, a police officer, an artist, a public servant, a poet, a professional writer, a spy—to share their recollections of these key experiences in their lives.

Our guiding philosophy is, surprisingly, nicely captured in the following meme:

> *You never really know the true impact you have on those around you. You never know how much someone needed that smile you gave them. You never know how much your kindness turned someone's entire life around. You never know how much someone needed that long hug or deep talk. So don't wait to be kind. Don't wait for someone else to be kind first. Don't wait for better circumstances or for someone to change. Just be kind, because you never know how much someone needs it.*

We're now collecting material for a volume III. If you'd like to participate, please contact either of us.

Harlan and Ed
Somewhere in Northeast Florida

Foreword

Finding a Meaning for One's Life
By Carol Spargo Pierskalla

In 2003 I had a major heart attack. At that time, I had to make a choice. As I lay on the floor of my bathroom hallway, I had to choose whether I would live or die. The choice was clear: if I pushed my Lifeline button, I would live; if I did not push it, I would die. There was no other help available other than the button. All the positives of dying – no more heart ache over children, no lingering illness, no watching my spouse die before me, no trying to figure out financial details – ran through my head. I hesitated.

Then another voice overrode that one, but it was as clear as the other voice: "You're not finished yet!"

So I pushed the button and chose life. Viktor Frankl in his book, *Man's Search for Meaning*, says we always have a choice. If we cannot choose different **external circumstances**, we can at least choose our **attitude** towards them.

And Dr. Frankl should know. He spent years in a Nazi concentration camp, the victim of religious persecution and plain old sadism. Yet through it all he maintained a stance of spiritual growth, seeing his suffering as having **meaning**. Those who did not find meaning (or purpose) in their circumstances, died. More than any other factor, he maintains that this is what kept him alive while his mother, father, brother and wife all perished. This does not mean that others cannot kill you. It only means that your suffering cannot kill you unless you let it.

After my heart attack I kept asking myself what the meaning was in my survival. Was I supposed to do some heroic act and save someone? Was I there so that I could greet a new daughter-in-law, three more grandchildren and five great grandchildren into my world?

"What is the **meaning** of your life?" Will that meaning stand the test of pain and suffering that may await you – or that may have already greeted you?

One older man who had lost his wife came to Frankl after the war suffering horribly in her absence. After listening to him, Frankl asked, "If you had died first, how would your wife have felt?" "She would have been in misery, just as I am," the man replied. "So you see," Frankl said, "by you surviving her, you are suffering in her place. She does not have to go through what you are going through." Frankl gave the man a **meaning** for his suffering.

Frankl is a psychiatrist who believes in spiritual growth. He talks of self-transcendence when others speak of self-actualization. I don't think we can ever be assured of our particular **meaning**; but we can take important steps forward, toward our meaning.

And this includes us all, even in our helplessness. When my mother was ill and dying, my brother, Jim, and my sister, Christine, and I figured out that since my mother could no longer participate in a conversation, we would meet in her room at the nursing home to converse with each other! So we met twice per week to share what was happening in our lives. We thought it was good for our relationships, but we didn't think about what effect it had on our mother. We had been talking of Christine going to hospital for something or other when Mom piped up with "What is Christine going to the hospital for?" Although she couldn't participate in our conversations, she was still listening!

My brother and sister and I have kept up the practice. Each October 2 (their birthdays and their wedding anniversary) we get together at their graves. We share hot chocolate, cookies and stories of how fortunate we were to have parents like they were. That was my mother's "**meaning**": she brought us closer together even when she was helpless in the nursing home.

Does your **meaning** have to do with your children? Grandchildren? A new home? A trip? It doesn't matter how unlikely it is (although it should be rooted in reality, not fantasy). Think about it! Pray about it! What is your **meaning**?

I MATTER TOO!

CHAPTER 1

The Age of Innocence: Childhood/ Elementary School

ഗ്രൂര

The Simple Act
By Dee Wallace

Sometimes life's smallest moments are life-changing. The bells don't clang, the fireworks don't explode. But simply, and quietly, someone does something that affects your life… for life. I had one of these experiences in my fifth-grade English class.

I know how teachers can affect the lives of their students. I have taught high school and had my own dance school and acting studio. I was always aware that, even in times of tough love, it is vitally important to teach with respect and honor the dignity of all students.

And thus, the story of how Ms. Eichorn, on a very normal day, in a very simple way, touched my heart and my life forever.

At the time, my family was living with my grandparents. We were poor, and my dad had a severe drinking problem which kept him from working. Growing up in my household was, at best, a dichotomy. There was always lots of love, but constant yelling and verbal abuse when Daddy would get too drunk. I was raised by two extraordinarily strong women: my mother and grandmother. They were my rocks. Grandma and Mom made sure we were given a good church upbringing. Mom did her best to create normalcy, and to do everything she could to ensure "the kids" were accepted into whatever the norm of acceptance was back then. In my memory, it was always about the money. We never had enough to really "fit in" in the circles that extended down into the popularity of high school competition. There was always this knowing that I "wasn't one of them".

I was talented enough and athletic enough that I made my own success somewhat: cheerleader and Homecoming Queen. Cheerleaders were chosen by merit, not popularity, and the teachers who oversaw the team actually voted on who received the honor. I owe my mom for that, too, because she bartered her secretarial services to get me dance lessons beginning at four. That helped create the athletic body that took me through the competitions. And Homecoming Queen? I always went out of my way to be nice and include everyone in the school. I think they just rallied around me and took me to victory. But, you see, inside me, I never really felt like I belonged. And that's where the change must happen: within us first.

Which brings me to Ms. Eichorn and the day we were reading aloud. It was my turn. I was ok at reading, although we never read much in our home. Everyone was just too busy making a living. I started my passage: "The dessert was beautiful this time of year." Everyone broke up in hysterical laughter. What? What had I done wrong? In seconds I was sliding down my chair and the old fear of "You don't belong!" surfaced up into my consciousness.

"Class!" Ms. Eichorn said gently but sternly, "Dessert and desert are spelled almost exactly the same way. Anyone can make mistakes like this, and it is not ok in my classroom for you to laugh and mock someone who is doing her best and trying." She turned to me with a smile. "The dry place with sand is spelled with one 's'. The delicious treat we have after dinner is spelled with two s's. Please proceed, Deanna."

Such a small moment. Such a seemingly insignificant happening in a young person's life. But in that moment, I felt seen, and heard, and that I belonged. I belonged.

After class, one of the cool boys in school came over to me to apologize. "We were stupid to do that," he said, "I hope you're ok." I smiled and thanked him. And then I went to Ms. Eichorn and hugged her. "Thank you for sticking up for me, Ms. Eichorn," It really meant a lot to me. She smiled and hugged me back. And just like that, the moment was over. A life-changing moment, nonetheless. I will always be grateful for the people who made me feel like I belonged. And now I get to choose that for myself… in every moment.

ℰℭ

Through the Eyes of a Child
By Jack Rawcliffe

A Bible, greeting cards, visits to strangers and a limp are four things when tied together become a picture of my mother's life of pain, hope, joy and completeness. When I was a youngster my earliest memories were of my mother sitting in her favorite chair next to the warm radiator and window. Early in the morning, after my father had gone to work, she would be reading the Bible. It was something she did all of her life. Sometimes she would read to me, but I was so young I don't really think I understood the words or the stories. I am sure I wasn't closely listening, but rather was just happy having her read to me and make me the center of her attention.

Another thing she did was send cards to people. They were sent not just at Christmas or on birthdays, but on any occasion. Happy Valentine Day, Happy Easter, Happy Springtime, get well, just thinking of you. Cards, Cards, Cards! I thought she kept the stores in business with all the cards. The cards went to people I didn't know. They were not our family, or people who came to our home. They weren't friends in the same way as our neighbors or people we saw at church on Sunday. I'm sure the cards were sent, because I made many trips to the blue mailbox at the end of our street.

When I was young in the 1950s, Sunday was a day we all went to church. When we came home it was a nice Sunday dinner and on occasion we would go for a drive. Sometimes we visited my grandfather, but every once in while we would visit one of the recipients of the cards. The trips were not fun for a youngster. These people lived in big buildings, like hospitals, except there weren't any doctors. The people we visited would smile at my mother when we appeared. My mother would parade my sister and me so the person could see how much we had grown since the last visit. One woman we visited had a great deal of difficulty speaking and sat in a wheelchair. It was uncomfortable for a youngster to endure these visits. One time I remember asking my dad, "Why do we have to come here?" "It makes your mother happy, so we do it. Someday you'll understand!" "But why do I have to show her how much I have grown?" At some point even a young boy learns when to stop asking questions. That time came and I went along on the visits without knowing why.

My family was always active, providing a good family environment. We went on vacations, to the beach, to amusement parks, etc. My mother participated in everything. At weddings or parties where there was music she would always dance with my dad. It seemed that there was a great deal of difficulty in dancing but she had a smile on her face, so she must have been enjoying herself. Everything seemed perfectly normal!

One day I was playing with a friend. He noticed my mother off in the distance, walking down the street. He said, "Hey, your mother's a cripple." I was about ten and knew what crippled meant, but I had never noticed.

As years go by, when more pieces of the puzzle of life seem to fit into place, I remember the Bible readings, the greeting cards, the visits and the limp. My mother's life started like most, with all the promise of fullness and happiness. There was a detour along the way. It led to a lot of pain and suffering, but also to faith and hope. That path brought me to be with those strangers who had been sent all those cards. It showed me that hope and faith can triumph. When I was paraded in front of those shut-ins, I now realize that it was not to show off, but rather to provide a measure of hope and fulfillment to those who had not been fortunate enough to get back on life's wonderful road like my mother. Maybe it was the words, hope, and promise she found every morning reading the Bible or maybe her faith that gave her a full life. She never forgot those with whom she had spent all those painful, hopeful years. She remembered them with the cards, the visits, the prayers and the hope she displayed through her full life.

As I look back at those years, there are memories that stay with you for a lifetime. For me the memories of my mother will be the Bible, greeting cards, visits to strangers and a limp. For my children and grandchildren, I share this story and many others. Maybe they will get to know and love this inspiring woman who was my mother. My hope is that they will realize that their values and character are in part a direct result of the effort she put into providing a good home for her family.

Valia Volpe was born in 1912, the sixth of twelve children. She spent most of her teen and young adult years in medical facilities for a disease of the hip which made walking without assistance almost impossible. Her medical problems necessitated that she attend the "School for Crippled Children" in Providence, Rhode Island, where she was one of its first graduates. She married at age 31 and had a full and happy life. She died in 2000 at the age of eighty-eight and was survived by her two children and seven grandchildren.

∾ℂ

She Loved Me Most; She Loved Me Best

By Sherry-Ann Morris

My mother's tenderness, clear sense of right and wrong, and desire for me to draw near to God go back to my earliest memories. Her love, sweetness, care, and character were like garments she wore permanently, deeply embedded into her core DNA. This is what she exuded and who she was through and through, even though her life had not been an easy one, especially as a child.

Mother had Typhoid Fever as a child and her father died of it. At the time they could not even tell her that her father had died, probably for fear of her not rallying herself. When she recovered from her illness, she found that she had lost out on a significant amount of her schooling, which resulted in her younger sister advancing beyond her. That was not to last for long, because she had made up her mind to catch up and take back her place, ahead of her sister, and so she did.

This desire to learn aggressively on demand is probably what set her up to become the intended of a young headmaster. He had no desire to marry young, but he merely saw the shadow of a person walking from an area enclosed by trees—a most beautiful landscape enshrouded by the best of God's beauty—and his mind was changed for him. A stone windmill behind him, and a person's shadow seen coming toward him from an enclave of trees, her intended at the time said something told him, "you're going to marry that person." His immediate response was to put that out of his mind; after all he was a young headmaster on a teaching assignment on an island which was not his home. Regardless, Mother came along that day, with no clue or interest in marrying yet herself. Nevertheless, marry young they did, and that was the beginning of their story.

They had eight children born – some miscarried along the way – and each one she loved significantly. One young son died of pneumonia, but the greater tragedy was that his caretaker was taking some of his food for her own child or children, weakening his immune system. I cannot imagine the pain she endured, and that of my family at the time, because I was not yet born. She said he was a beautiful child. The child born after him was also exceptionally beautiful and with a small nose. Later, she wondered if she was prideful in thinking the next child so beautiful, and if perhaps his challenges were a punishment for her delight in her beautiful baby boy who lived; so cruel is the one who torments the children of God. She spent many years travailing in prayer for the beautiful child born after her son with pneumonia died.

These things help explain the depth of some of her challenges in life. Her mother-in-law did not love her. Her mother-in-law had likely wanted someone whose family rank and position were higher than Mother's, as the man Mother married was of great intelligence, his grandfather was well-off, and they likely had other plans for him, but not so God. The same woman who did not love my mother, and who did not treat her well in the early stages of their marriage, received my mother's great care and love in the latter part of her life. Mother cared for her as she aged and could no longer do for herself what she once could.

Mother's love was always higher; she always gave what people did not deserve. As a teenager, I definitively planned not to be like her in that regard. People could be so awful at times—in fact very wicked—therefore firm and swift justice would be best for their evil ways, period. I was young, not overly patient and had no room then for entertaining such grace. That kind of heart did not seem to make sense to me. Yet Mother experienced many challenges and helped many people. Her home welcomed cousins, a nephew, or distant family members, as they lived in her already full home of up to seven children, depending on the time. Still, she hosted these dear teens and young adults for several years at a time and showed each one complete love; that was simply her way. Constant love was given, but she was tough and firm when she had to be, which is another form of love though often only later understood.

Mother later endured a bout with cancer and was victorious over it; she said she wanted to be around to see me graduate – she lived well beyond that season and attended two of my graduations. She lost her beloved husband later in life, of whom she said she would have married a thousand times over, so great was her love for him. She nursed him, along with her eldest daughter, while his body grew weak. She never complained but counted it a privilege every day he was with her and she could serve him.

Mother faced many storms and lost not one because her victories were internal as she served the Risen One. She was a woman of deep, constant, selfless prayer for whomever and whenever. These things frame her life and help you understand the gift she gave.

Mother was a midwife and a nurse, in the Caribbean and in Connecticut. She worked at a mental health center, as a nurse, among other hospitals and facilities. She loved the people at the mental health facility dearly and she did not hold their at times brutish ways against them. She cared about them and respected them; even when the guards were fearful for her well-being during one incident, she was not afraid and wanted to be left to care for the man in need despite his previous actions. "Perfect love casts out all fear (I John 4:18);" this comes to mind when remembering this story.

My mother gave to me the gift of example. It is a rare, honorable, timeless gift still with me today. She made it her ongoing business to point me to the One in whom I would find all I ever need – the King of kings and Lord of lords. She modeled love and forgiveness, sharing and caring, understanding and grace. She did not manipulate others to get her way or hold things against people, even if their actions or inaction deserved otherwise. She never complained; she did not tell of her weariness or how others failed her, nor did she berate those who may have deserved some berating – that was not her way. She chose a higher way of loving, giving, and being. Her way is so rare; I know few like her, so honorable and kind was she.

She was also incredibly funny, and she loved to laugh; she never lost her ability to tell jokes. As for her standards, oh they were so remarkably high, in anything and everything she did – cleaning, cooking, sewing, baking, and working in her chosen occupation. She was a lover, and I believe as a lover she expected the best of one's talents to be used at all times; therefore, everything she did needed to match the greatness of the love God showed to her and that which she showed back to Him.

So you will better understand what she did for me, she did not do it in one day or one week; she did it over her lifetime. She depicted godly grace, truthfulness, and boldness. She was who she was everywhere she went. It was her desire for me to love God, to choose Him, and to serve Him for myself. As for serving Him, even there it was with a freedom to do so not as she thought I should and her plans for my life, but as He guided and directed me; again, so unselfish was she. It was not about her agenda for my life, it was so that I, through loving Him, would find mine in the life He has gifted and destined for me.

Along with my father, my mother afforded me every opportunity to grow and become who I am and am still becoming. Together, they sacrificed easy retirement in their lands and home country by moving to another country late in life so that I my siblings and I could have the benefits and opportunities that life in the United States would afford us.

I treasure forever the gift of being the best her she could be and then intentionally teaching me the Way of the Master, making the Word of God come alive to me, and praying me through countless storms. My mother directed my life to face due North—it is an incomprehensible gift she has given me. I can never repay it because I have experienced tremendous joy and gifts unfathomable that only a God can give, and my spirit is connected to an eternal God—and what and who can ever compare to this?

There were things she did not choose, like when they wanted my father to run for politics in our home country—promotions, gifts, and ease of life would have come with this, but there would have been either much compromise or travail in not compromising. She advised my father against this, which was to my great benefit; I am not so sure I would have been born to them otherwise. I am glad they left small island politics to those with a taste for it. Then there were all the international trips she did not take with my father because she wanted to directly oversee the safety and well-being of her children by staying at home and not leaving them in the care of another. There were many things she went without, so her children could have more. Countless meals were forfeited when my father would bring home yet another unexpected guest, so my siblings tell me. The example she was, without ever trying to be, indeed I am so thankful for who she was—Mother, sister, and best friend.

The entire course of my life and what it will be has been irrevocably altered by the grace, love, and character witnessed, admired, and now better understood by me.

The best part is that she now lives again, for the spirit man lives forever and takes up its spiritual body when we chose Christ. Many may think that we go to some sort of frozen rest, but that it not the case. We enter an expanse that our hearts can barely imagine, and there is much work to be done there, too—rich and great assignments to partake of with God, centuries old and eternity past—so there is also a lot of catching up to do and much to understand, examine, take hold of, and behold. Whilst leaning in to perceive new glories unfolding, His ever-changing magnificence, and having the ability and positioning to peek into His splendor and communicate with the One who knows all, we get to be in His presence firsthand to truly know of His ways. What, oh what, can compare to all of this? This unfathomable glory story will really just begin; this life pales in comparison to there, but this is after all what we know for now. We are thankful to be here and in so being to receive every blessing and hidden treasure, but there is no way our forever home is not infinitely better than what we experience and know here, less than one percent, of one percent, of one percent. Anyway, I am ever so thankful to know all that she is experiencing there—though parted—part bliss to know she is in perfection, wanting nothing, and in the full action of all things—still. How magnificent—selah!

My mother's prayers still speak, and I believe her desire for people of all nations to know Christ is still active. I know she would want all who read this and have not yet made a choice to invite the Giver of Life into their life to do so now—yes, today—to not be wishy washy or weak minded and afraid, and even if you are, to buck up anyway and choose the One who loves you most and who loves you best—Jesus Christ of Nazareth.

~

This article is dedicated to Constance Madeline Morris for she is the one of all people I know who has loved me most, in every way

Constance Madeline Morris at her daughter's birthday outing celebration – always royal and always a trooper, even when going out became more challenging.

possible, and she has loved me best, in every way imaginable and even when not deserved. Most importantly, she introduced me to the One, who would change everything in my life through His glorious life. Knowing Him, His ways so vast, His boundaries so limitless; it is as though I am still just beginning to know this Christ and I am forever grateful that she was here and blessed to know now there.

ℰℭ

The Job I Never Wanted
By Tracy Tripp

The one job I never wanted was that of a teacher. Why? For one reason, some of the teachers in my hometown, on occasion, acted more like the students than the professionals they should have been—or so rumors led me to believe. Maybe they were all just that—rumors, but something tells me otherwise. Another reason I did not want to be a teacher was that I believed that in some way, if I became a teacher I would be stuck in a phase of my life. I would forever be in the school system and never springing forth into the world full of all the careers that schooling was meant to prepare me for.

I entered college unsure of my future and settled on majoring in accounting. A few semesters in, I realized that accounting was not going to be my thing, either. Call it divine intervention, but I spoke to my counselor, changed my major, and began classes to become…yes, a teacher. I can't explain how the decision happened. It just did. I excelled in these classes, unlike accounting.

After graduating, I landed a job as a middle school science teacher. Becoming a teacher was a second opportunity for me to embrace the subject matter as a mature adult that realized that, yes, I did want to know a great deal of that stuff that seemed so boring at the time. I found I loved learning, and I wanted to share that love of learning with the students. But much like a new parent, I felt I had so much to prove. Had I mastered the subject myself? Could I make learning fun? And the question that worried me most—could I manage a classroom?

After six years, I believe I was handling myself sufficiently and didn't see anything but improvement and more years of meeting new students in my future. Then I had my first baby, fell madly in love with motherhood, and after one year, decided to stay home and have two more babies. As they grew, I dabbled with teaching in their preschool and working with small groups through Title I.

Then another life change brought me back to being a stay-at-home mom. We moved to Florida. My husband and I decided I should take a year off and make sure everyone adjusted to the move. Eight years went by, four novels and two children's books were published, and the idea of standing in front of a classroom of students again was far from my mind.

Again, life had plans other than the ones I expected. I began subbing for grades K-12. I was amazed how natural the position felt, and even more surprised that instead of the time away diminishing my ability, years of living had made me more confident.

My journey with teaching has been interesting and surprising, but maybe the one fact that has surprised me more than any other is that I started my journey with a lack of respect for teachers—feeling they were somehow stuck in their youth, holding fast to the "If you can't do—teach" mentality. But my journey has made me realize how very hard teachers work and how important their job is in this world.

After raising three children, and growing in my faith, I step into a classroom knowing that the children that hate to be there, that cannot sit in their seats for over ten minutes with jumping up to do some unnecessary task is not just a parent's child, but a child of God as well. The ones without their supplies because they couldn't remember to put them in their bag even though the supplies were sitting on the counter—well, that might have been my child at one point or another. The one sent to the dean for being too impulsive, yeah—I might have raised one like that. The one feeling anxious, depressed, overwhelmed—yup, I've got one of those as well.

Every year, I prayed each one of my children landed in the classroom led by a teacher that loved kids, knew their subject matter, and taught with enthusiasm. I prayed that when their teacher's day seemed overwhelming, that teacher would turn to the patience of God and not to the emotions fueled by anger and feelings of defeat.

Did my kids come home from school and tell me, "They didn't teach that?" Yes. Did I believe them and wonder what was going on the classroom? Yes. I did that, too. But as a sub, I bounce from classroom to classroom, to school to school, and what I mostly see are amazing people trying so very hard to do remarkable things for children that belong to them for only a short time. These are not people stuck in the past, never graduating from a school system, they are holding the torch for a brighter tomorrow. They are the parents, the leaders, the role models of generations of children. They touch more lives than so many other professions. They aren't rewarded with incredible incomes. Their rewards are little notes of thanks and occasional sweets from the PTA.

I'm grateful to be a substitute teacher. The opportunity allows me to see the struggle and successes of a profession that too often is under-appreciated and taken for granted. Thinking back to the years my children have been in school, I realize that I owe many teachers more gratitude than I ever showed them. So, to all the teachers that have given our children their everything — thank you! You truly do have one of the most important jobs.

ℰᴏᴄᴋ

Skunk Oil Skills
By Ruth Van Alstine

My Dad used to tell us stories of his childhood. His tales of the old days were fascinating because they came from a very different kind of world. He was born in 1910, back when they used horse and wagon to deliver milk cans to the creamery and hunted squirrels for dinner. He had all kinds of stories up his sleeve for our entertainment. There was one tale he told that sticks in my mind to this day which summarizes his core values and how he looked at the world, how he thought people should treat one another. It was intertwined in the middle of his memoirs of how he earned extra money when he was very young.

Part of his money-making endeavors were that he would trap animals for their pelts and then sell them. For this particular story, he added on a new dimension, that of a special skill he was particularly adept at, which involved skunks. Now, you might ask yourself, what on earth would you want to trap a skunk for? His answer was simple, their oil. Apparently, the local doctor used this skunk oil to make a poultice for patients who had chest ailments like pneumonia or congestion issues. But, he went on to explain, you had to know how to remove the oil sac just so as not to break it, and he was really good at this particular skill, and boasted, was actually the best in the area. He continued with a story of how he had once saved the lives of two large, strapping young men who were twins and lived down the road from his family on a nearby farm. My Dad had kept the local doctor supplied with skunk oil and after the twins had contracted a particularly severe case of pneumonia, the doctor had used his skunk oil in poultices to cure their pneumonia, and so, Daddy felt he had saved their lives and was proud of that fact, that he was able to do that with his skill at extracting skunk oil for the doctor.

Thinking this story was associated with his extra money earning efforts (since the story was told while we were talking about that), I said to him, "You must have made a lot of money, selling that skunk oil to the doctor." He looked at me pointedly, and sternly, as if disciplining me as a small child again, and simply stated, "I never would make money off of the skunk oil, I gave it to him to make medicine, that's what we did in those days, it was the right thing to do." That is what the old values were, look out after your neighbors. Yes, you had to survive and worked your butt off to earn a few pennies, but when it came to supporting the community, like giving the doctor supplies for medicine to save lives, you gave that freely, and didn't expect or want a penny in return.

ॐ☙

A New Landscape
By Sally Wahl Constain

Never ending hills roll on,
searching for the illusive
ever moving horizon.
We find ourselves in a new realm.
Danger lurks around and beyond
every crooked corner.
We are isolated, and yet connected.
We are one with the
unifying universe.
Calls of concern come in from
Colombia, Arizona, Oneonta.
Childhood friends from the past
appear in the present.
A message out of the blue
from Farzana, a former
second grade student,
suddenly summons me,
thanking me for teaching poetry
and making a difference.
Now a nurse,
she is heeding the desperate call to arms
like so many in her field.
What can we do?
Pray for the safety of all, and
conjure up our inner resources
to create
while we wait,
and wash our hands.

Notes for your memories of this age:

I MATTER TOO!

CHAPTER 2

The Age of Learning: High School/ College

ഓരു

How a Police Officer Made a Difference in One Person's Life
By Mal MacIver

Many years ago, I read Mitch Albom's *The Five People You Meet in Heaven*. Although no one can say if there is a Heaven, I have no doubt that each of us has been influenced by many people and at our age we have influenced many people. We can only hope that most of those influences have been positive.

Most cops, if you can get them to talk, will describe big cases or investigations that they were involved in during their careers as we all have them if we were on the job long enough. Here's not a big case, but what would be considered a minor case that nonetheless influenced a young girl's life.

At the time I was assigned in the juvenile bureau of the Derry, New Hampshire police department as a juvenile officer. As such I worked cases of youths that had run afoul of the law. I was fortunate to have discretion in the resolution of these cases before the court. I worked closely with the courts' probation officers and we all agreed that our goal was not to punish but to reform antisocial behavior. Now that's not to say that all cases could be resolved this way because they weren't and many times incarceration was necessary for the protection of the child as well as society.

Back to the case I mentioned. This case originally came in from a drug arrest. Through investigation, I learned of a difficult home environment and a child acting out by the use of narcotics. This was not a unique case and basically was unremarkable. This child had several siblings and all were vulnerable. By getting school resources, drug counselors, and the court to approve an action plan that we had developed and being supervised by the probation department, this case was completed as far as I was concerned.

My career moved on, and I was promoted through the ranks with various assignments. About ten years later, my wife who was a realtor was dealing with another realtor. Unknown to my wife this realtor was the child mentioned above. When she recognized my wife's last name she asked if she was related to me. After confirming that I was her spouse, she explained to my wife that I had changed the course of her life many years before. She was now a very successful businesswoman and respected in her profession.

I would love to be able to say that I had kept track of her case and monitored her progress, however that was not true. At the time there was a large case load and we all tried to do what we thought was beneficial for the child. In this case, the system worked.

ℰ❀ℭ

Inspiration, Thy Name is Marion
By Jim Meskimen

I've been very fortunate to have run across many inspirational people. The thing I find about inspiring people is that they are keen on sharing their methods; they don't keep it a secret.

Others may be dazzling, but the truly inspirational share the route, the method of walking their path. They may be miles and miles ahead, almost out of sight in some cases, but you still can get an idea of their humble beginnings, and what fuels them to move forward.

I've been doubly lucky to have as an inspiration my own mom, who happens to be an award-winning actress. Marion Ross, who gained fame as Ron Howard's TV mom in Happy Days, is my biological, actual mom. (I think I got the better end of that bargain. Ron had his own terrific mom, Jean, whom I knew and admired, too.)

I witnessed Marion deal with the challenges of being a working actress while raising two kids as a single mom. Even though at the time, I wasn't particularly sympathetic to the many burdens she carried, I look back now in utter amazement.

The thing I think I gained the most from observing was her attitude of commitment; she never backed down from her dream of being a working, important actress. She also never backed down from her goal of helping my sister and me to be raised safely, comfortably, and prepared for life.

Doing one of these things might be considered challenging enough; doing both is a huge accomplishment.

She set a great example, always, of professionalism and hard work. Both my sister and I have followed her into show business; my sister Ellen Kreamer as a writer/producer, and I as an actor, and our enthusiasm (or at least tolerance) for hard work comes directly from our mom's example.

She would often be found cooking dinner or cleaning the kitchen while running lines for an audition or a role, or hustling out to brave the freeway into Hollywood to do some last-minute interview, making sure we had something to eat, and clean clothes.

We never wanted for anything in our home, and it was due to her diligence and ambition.

When my wife and I were raising our own child, and I could really appreciate the amount of work and attention and pure hustle it takes to raise a child in today's world, I marveled at how well Marion managed to do it all by herself.

Marion is in her nineties now, and retired from acting, but she still inspires all of us in our family every day with her humor and her spirit of fun and discovery. She is every bit the youngster from Albert Lea, Minnesota that dreamed of a glamorous career in Hollywood, despite all odds, now content in the knowledge that she won the game she set out to play.

𝕊𝕆ℂ𝕉

Only If I
By Kathy Triebwasser

I sit down to fill my belly with salty chips and pineapple salsa. A bowl of crisp lettuce, grilled chicken, Mexican cheese with a dollop of homemade ranch dressing and guacamole sits waiting, to be my lunch on the run.

I hear a tone in a conversation next to me that makes my skin crawl. I really do not want to hear this. I just want to eat, clear my e-mails, look at places to rent in Los Angeles, and move on with my day easily.

A young woman sits two tables away on the opposite side of the table next to me. She has purple highlights in her dark black shoulder-length straight hair. Her nose is pierced with a silver stud. Her tattoos on her arms get my attention. She is wearing a white shirt and black pants. My best guess is she is about 18 years old. A shabby, disheveled, older male is sitting across the table.

"When are you going to finish school?" he asks.

"When I get a chance."

"What's up with your mom?"

"She's okay."

"Has Sally been staying over?"

"I don't know."

"What's up with your brother?"

"He's the same."

"Did Jerry and Jess come by?'

"Yes, they're fine."

"You know you need to go to school. You will never make anything of yourself if you don't finish school. Are you working? You're supposed to be working"

"Yes, I am working. I like my job."

"So how much are they paying you at that job you like?"

"I am hoping to be able to shampoo people soon."

"What do you mean they won't let you shampoo anyone's hair?"

"You know I went through tough times, too. I had to struggle to make ends meet in my life. You can do better than this."

Finally it stops; he takes a bite out of his burrito.

She says, "I have to babysit all the time. When I walk in the door, Mom says 'you can watch her.' She then disappears for hours. I will take care of her until she goes to bed." He says nothing.

I am trying to keep my eyes focused on my food and phone. I glance up a few times. Her face goes from blank, to grimace, to disgust and back again so many times I cannot keep up. It's like watching an endless volley in a tennis match.

The large burly man with the mustache, unkempt brown hair, t-shirt, shorts, dirty sandals that is sitting across from her is deaf and blind to her. He keeps rolling along like a steam roller over hot asphalt. She endures.

Divorced Dad's visit of week, month or maybe even year is torture. He is trying to care, to be involved, to influence his daughter. Cramming a parental connection in thirty minutes is like stuffing a five pound suitcase with fifty pounds of stuff.

"We need to see each other more often, you need to call me, or ask to see me," he says with a demanding tone.

She looks up at him "I think people should know you care about them without having to spend time with them, without talking to them, or calling them. I tell all my friends that just because I don't call them, doesn't mean I don't care about them."

Dad says nothing, looks at the floor; an awkward silence occurs. Wow, that says it all. She is slamming the door.

I can empathize. I would like to run for cover. If only I could have sidestepped hearing this conversation. I keep my head down. I avoid making eye contact with her. I don't want her to see my distress. My stomach is churning. It's not from my lunch.

If only she could have said, "Wait a minute, Dad, you're not paying attention, not listening, not seeing the damage you're creating." She is invisible to him. A young girl who hasn't found her voice.

I bet nobody told him that he needed to relate to his daughter, not berate her. He would be totally shocked to realize how miserably he is blowing it. The young woman has no one. She gives up the fight and takes the escape route. She knows he has nothing to give.

If only I had reordered this interaction. I would play it back for them. I could pause it at the moments when it all went up in smoke. Maybe I could get them to try it again. Maybe with another try they could start the fire again, warm this up, to something above freezing.

I know where you are, young woman. I was there myself. People in my life either neglected or rode hard on me, too. No parent or grandparent was there for me. I hate to sound whiny. I was a white, upper middle class female, living in a clean home, with good food on the table, and nice clothes. I was privileged in most people's eyes. I lived in a house of plenty with nobody home.

Did I have a huge piece missing in life? You betcha. I felt it then but could not have told you what it was. I see it clearly as I watch it play out in front of my eyes today.

Coming of age for me was a minefield of missteps. I made a mess of my life for many years. Who knows if only I had someone growing up who had been there for me, could it have been different, maybe or maybe not?

My third grade teacher, Mrs. Floyd, was so sweet to me. She was pretty in an unassuming way. She had soft brown hair, small frame, graceful hands and walked with a limp. I loved her soft voice and sweet smile. She never raised her voice to me. Her gentle way touched me deeply.

In fourth grade Mrs. Teuton found I was way behind in spelling. Mrs. Teuton was tall, gawky, and loud, nothing like Mrs. Floyd. She was a no-nonsense teacher.

"Mrs. Floyd didn't teach you anything," railed my Mom. My heart sank, my face burned with anger. I loved Mrs. Floyd. She was the first adult that was kind to me.

Mrs. Teuton asked my mother to work on my spelling with me. The first night she tried I totally froze. I was so afraid of her. I could not spell a single word. "You can do better than this. What is the matter with you? You are not even trying! I give up." The spelling book in her right hand came crashing down on my head.

My mother walked away in disgust. She called Mrs. Teuton immediately. I sat on the living room couch too scared to move. I could hear her talking on her bedroom phone. "I cannot work with her. Is she stupid or something? What's wrong with her? She is totally not trying. I lost my temper and hit her over the head with the book."

Mrs. Teuton must have replied "I will take care of it. Stop working with her."

Mrs. Teuton, the woman who saved me from my mother's harsh tutoring, put me in the dummy spelling group, which made me learn to spell. Mrs. Floyd was sweet and Mrs. Teuton was sour but put the two together with my own desire to succeed, it worked enough to get by.

I see in that young girl someone who looks so different from me. We share a life experience that makes us one. I hope that she has had or will have a Mrs. Floyd and a Mrs. Teuton at some point in her life. They will fill a gap. The rest will be up to her.

If only I could say to that young girl: You will learn you are enough. You will see things differently. You will always have someone there for you. I know you won't always get an "if only" but you will always get an "only if I".

A Walk with Janis Joplin
By Elaine Chekich

Somehow I have a knack for meeting well-known, exciting people. I'm not sure why, being at the right place at the right time, I suppose, like some kind of offbeat physics. So, while I may not present the air of any particular specialness, I do have the talent of meeting famous people.

Like the time I encountered Janis Joplin. She was singing off the flatbed of a Hertz rent-a-truck in San Francisco's Golden Gate Park. I was thirteen and lived nearby. Both my parents worked so, unmonitored, unfiltered, I roamed the park after school and on the weekends, looking for adventure, which most of the time took the form of high school boys foisting cigarettes on me.

Janis wore a feathered, fuchsia hat, her torso swathed in yellow and orange boas over a loose lavender vest. Her blousy pants were made of silky parachute material. Bands playing in the park were no big deal at the time. It was a free spot to rehearse and blow out the lungs and shrieking guitars. This was before Joplin and her band, Big Brother and the Holding Company, had made it, so no fans collected. They were nobodies, just like me.

Joplin was an extraordinary singer. She gave everything she had, vocally, emotionally, physically, even at a routine rehearsal. Though my 13-year-old brain didn't process her gift in so many words, I recognized that, as Janis turned beet red, hunching her body, writhing to expel notes of a bluesy lament, she was astronomically raw and uncontained by this world. Her performance was one thousand percent genuine. I'd never seen a human being like Joplin. Glistening molecules appeared to collect and light her aura of youthful fragility and insupportable bravery as if she might die any moment from the effort.

I was dazzled. She could see that in my eyes, I'm sure. Maybe that's why she talked to me. She smiled a crooked smile, wiping off perspiration and flouncing her clothes to aerate. "Why aren't you in school, baby doll?" She had the same drawl as my Texas-born mother.

"It's Saturday."

"Is it? Those damn days do slide 'long, don't they? Ever get to Haight?"

I was taken aback. "I don't hate. My mom says hate is Satan-inspired." She stared at me, bewildered and then dissolved into racking laughter.

In fact, Janis meant the intersection of the streets Haight and Ashbury that would become the global address of the great sixties' bands and hippie counterculture. It was close to Golden Gate Park, though a few years before the Haight achieved its Hippie Chic.

"Girl, you're funny. Haight is a street. Com' on," her voice cracked, "I gotta take a breather." She slipped on a longish jacket as we went.

We walked in a zigzag manner as if tag-teaming eucalyptus and pine trees. Squirrels angled down the trunks. "Oh," Janis exclaimed, "give 'em some," inexplicably pulling peanuts-in-the-shell from her jacket.

She tossed a few, and so did I. Brash squirrels whacked the shells and then danced away with them. "Far out!" Her loud laugh caused flocks of blackbirds to lift out of the trees. Our camaraderie was so natural. I dreamed of her being my big sister. Her star was bright, and I felt mine rising.

We walked back to the Hertz truck where the guys were packing up. They had to do a soundcheck somewhere. She hugged me with her frizzy hair and big voice. "Keep bein' real, darlin'," and stepping to the truck, she disappeared into the kaleidoscope of rock fame.

I was a sophomore at the University of California, Berkeley, when I heard that Janis Joplin had been found dead. I was nineteen, about the age of the young singer when I met her in the park. I felt deep sorrow. Her era of blues, boas, and feathered hats had come to an end. I remembered our walk when I took my first steps toward leaving childhood. I wanted to do important things in life, and Janis was my earliest model. She showed me I didn't have to be an invisible girl. Yes, she was flawed, but at the same time, she taught me the lesson of being an artist, of having faith in commitment.

Joplin gave it everything she had, all the time, and she lives on in favored skies as the example of a girl from Port Arthur, Texas, who dared to make it against the odds.

Notes for your memories of this age:

I MATTER TOO!

CHAPTER 3

The Age of Responsibility: Adulthood

⁊Ω

Birthdays
By Buzz Williams

This is a story of two birthdays. I was born William Otto Williams, III on October 18, 1948 at Bolling Air Force Base in Washington, D.C.

I spent the years between birthdays living a life that was pretty average and uneventful except that our family moved a lot as my father was a career Air Force NCO. We grew up in a home where our parents worked long hours in addition to cooking, cleaning, and taking care of everything else. As with most families during that time, the children took care of each other and as the oldest sibling, I became a responsible adult at a young age. What there wasn't any time for was Church, much less daily Bible study, but we didn't know any better because my father was far from a role model for Christian living. We just thought that was the way everyone lived. Occasionally, my mother would drop me off at 7th Avenue Baptist Church in Gastonia, North Carolina to attend Sunday School and then pick me up afterwards or we might dress up and go to Church for a funeral. You might say we were CEOs (Christmas and Easter Only).

Preparations for my second birth started when I married Mary Elizabeth Player on November 11, 1967. A beautiful, kind, caring, generous, and loving Christian woman, who invested years of time and energy to put me on and keep me on the right path as I battled those two traits that hamper one's progress: being easily distracted, and if that wasn't bad enough, procrastination. After 32 wonderful years of marriage, Mary went home on September 11, 1999 to be with her family and prepare a place for me. GOD answered my prayers and blessed me with another soul mate, Beverly, who also faces challenges with my bad traits but that's a tale for another book.

Back to this story. As I was driving home from a business trip in October 1982 I was "shot in the back". Or at least I thought I was. I remember it well! I was driving my new 1982 Buick LeSabre four-door sedan with super-soft seats the size of a couch. I pulled off to the side of the road, screaming in pain, opened the driver's side door and rolled out onto the paved emergency lane. I somehow managed to inspect the seat for blood but found none, crawled back into the car, and proceeded to the first doctor's office I could find. Keep in mind this was after regular working hours and there wasn't such a thing as a doc-in-a-box on every street corner. I found an open doctor's office and blew my car horn for what seemed like forever until the nurse eventually came out with a wheelchair. The doctor looked at me and immediately announced "you will survive, it's only a kidney stone." Easy for him to say, he wasn't the one trying to shove a big jagged rock through small paper-thin skin in a sensitive area. At the time, it didn't seem like I was going to survive so I did what everybody does — pray and promise to go to church if GOD will get them through this ordeal. With Mary pushing and dragging, I kept my promise the following Sunday as I ran to the front of the church when the invitation was given and was Baptized that night. I was Reborn, a saved Child of GOD on October 10, 1982 at Parkwood Baptist Church in Jacksonville, Florida.

My life has significantly improved since making that decision and our family has been blessed beyond all expectations. I'm eternally grateful that GOD is an important part of my life and he selected a hammer rather than an axe to get my attention on that faithful day.

Philippians 4:13, I can do all things through Him who strengthens me.

෨෮

Priorities
By Sam Roberts

It was May 2002. A beautiful evening. I was taking orders and serving the hundreds of moms, dads, and their kids at the annual Carnival food tent — a fundraiser our church organized every year for parishioners and townspeople from nearby surrounding communities. Working alongside me was another father, like myself, a man I was fortunate enough to meet a few years earlier for no other reason except our kids went to the same parochial school. As our kids became friends, so did we. Good friends. The kind of friend you respect and know you can trust. One who will always tell you the truth — their truth without judgement.

That said, everyone has at least one 'what's it all about, Alfie' moment in their life. Some may call it a crossroad, a happening, or an event. I was having mine and my friend was there to lend an ear. On our break from the food tent I pulled him aside and said, "Can I talk to you about something? I have a problem and I need some advice." I began to hem and haw my way through the first couple of sentences—not really knowing how to begin. He gently put his hand on my shoulder and said, "Sam, life is pretty easy. You only have three priorities. Faith, family, and work. That's it. Any problems that arise can always be solved because it's going to involve two of those three priorities." He went on to explain, "Take family and work—it could be you are working too much and you don't spend enough time with your wife and kids. Or take faith and work. You might have an awesome opportunity to make a lot of money and climb that ladder but in order to do so you're going to have to hurt a lot of people to get there. And then there's family and faith. Maybe you are keeping secrets from the ones you love, or cheating on your wife. So I don't need to know what your problem is because the answer lies in your priorities. Get them straight and the answer will follow."

I spent some time thinking about what he'd said and realized something about myself. I was rock solid when it came to family and work, but my faith was noncommittal. I was born Jewish and grew up in a Jewish home. As a young boy/man, I was sent to a Christian school while studying for my Bar Mitzvah. Years later I moved to New York, fell in love, married a Catholic woman, and promised to raise my kids Catholic. I dutifully went to Mass every Sunday with my family for the first 14 years of our marriage. I would sit in the pew trying to believe in and talk to God while everyone else was taking communion. I was going through the motions and doing a pretty good job of it, too.

But faith, as much as I wished/wanted it to be, wasn't really a priority.

In April 2003, my good friend from the carnival tent died suddenly. He was 40 years old—five years younger than me. I went into an emotional tailspin. I kept thinking of him, the three priorities, and 'what's it all about, Alfie?' For the first time in my life I was lost and alone even though I had a beautiful family who loved me, and a wonderful career for my work. But, I had lost my faith—probably because I never really had any.

Somewhere during this time of sadness I was inspired to enroll into the R.C.I.A (Rite of Christian Initiation of Adults) program through our church. Simply put, because I needed to get to know God. In April 2004, at Easter Vigil, I was baptized Catholic. In the fall of 2005, I was asked by one my dearest friends (a man I believe with all my heart to be on loan from God) to be his 'wing-man' and help him in his youth ministry. For the next 15 years, every other Sunday, we'd meet with high schoolers in our church meeting room. It was one of the greatest experiences/gifts/blessings in my life. But that story is for another time…

Thinking back on that evening at the carnival, I truly don't remember what it was I wanted to talk to my friend about and honestly, it doesn't really matter. I'm just forever grateful I did. Finally, I got my three priorities straight and life is pretty easy. Thanks be to God.

ℰℭ

From the City Block to the Cell Block
By Patrick Collins

Walking down a corridor inside a maximum-security prison while the population is "moving" is an experience I wasn't prepared for. The term simply means that there are hundreds of men walking in the corridors on the other side of a line heading in the opposite direction just two feet away. The men are moving either back to their cells from dinner or to the yard or to attend any of the many evening programs.

My friend John had recently started volunteering in a program called RTA (Rehabilitation Through the Arts) which was bringing the arts into prisons. The program was putting on plays inside the prison with the prisoners. As it turned out RTA was much more than putting on plays.

As facilitators we were teaching conflict resolution, creative writing, public speaking, and a myriad of other life skills that would help the men while incarcerated and certainly if and when they would return to society.

Upon arrival in our classroom there were 28 men, all of color and all twice my size in girth, all having taken full advantage of the free weights in the yard. My friend says, "I'll be right back," and left for 20 minutes.

There I was alone, and thus began 14 glorious years of volunteering inside Green Haven Correctional Facility, an experience that changed my life forever.

It took a while but slowly the men started to trust us. They would ask "Why would you give up two nights a week (sometimes more when we were in production) to be with us. You could be anywhere." When they realized that we were there because we believed in them, something miraculous happened, their souls overflowed with gratitude, honesty, vulnerability. It is often said that inside a prison everyone has to hide their real feelings for fear of anyone taking advantage of them, their guard always up, hiding behind a mask. When they enter RTA they leave that mask at the door.

Two quick stories: One night we were sitting around talking when 'P,' a light skinned African American man with freckles across his nose, started, "You know I grew up in the Bronx. My father wasn't in the picture. My mother was constantly comparing me to everyone else and I wasn't measuring up. I got tired of it. I went around the block and what was around the block were gangs, guns, violence and drugs… and that's how I ended up here."

In the silence, I jumped in "You know I, too, grew up in the Bronx. I, too, had a father who wasn't in the picture and my mother compared me to other people and I, too, didn't measure up and I, too, got tired of it and I, too, went around the block but what was around the block for me was a church, Saint Nicholas of Tolentine, a positive faith community that involved all of us in sports and other worthwhile endeavors. Because of that experience, I ended up in the seminary for six years… and that's how I ended up here."

Again silence.

Maybe, just maybe, it's what's around the block that makes all the difference.

The other story is from one of the RTA fundraisers. It was a beautiful evening with friends of RTA and some formerly incarcerated (alumni) along with some family members of men still inside. Toward the end of the evening a woman came over to me and introduced herself as the mom of one of our guys. Her son had been in our latest production. Each production is filmed and the DVD sent home to the families. As the woman approached, I could see she was fighting back her emotions. She said that she had received the DVD. She added, "My son was always on the street. I tried everything to get him off but to him, everything was the streets. He was 17 when he went away and this play and this DVD," she continued, now with tears flowing freely down her faces and dropping from her jaw line. "This play and this DVD, this was the first time I got to be proud of my son."

Throughout the years the men wrote and performed many plays, all with themes such as forgiveness, redemption, conflict resolution, isolation, and self-worth. There are many troubled people in prison and many of them have done some very bad things. Some have been wrongfully accused. Some received sentences that had they been white or had resources, they would have likely gotten off with self-defense and no time or minimal time. The system is broken. If you honestly think about it, the deck seems to be so stacked against them. Their family situation and what was "around the block" was too strong a pull to give a young man a sense of belonging which we all crave. Some 88% of all prisoners in the State of New York come from six different neighborhoods in New York City. Right out of the gate they don't have much of a chance.

Almost all of the men in our program landed in prison between the ages of 17 and 21 and most of the crimes were related in some way to drugs. Many experts agree that the decision-making part of the brain doesn't fully develop until the age of 25.

But 95% of all prisoners will someday go home, so why not help them, rehabilitate them, so that when they do go home, they can be productive members of society.

Every night when I leave the prison and get in my car in the parking lot outside of these massive walls, it hits me that this was a night well spent. I say to myself: I was with the Lord tonight and I feel blessed.

ഇ⊙ൽ

A Nudge and a Will
By Ruth Van Alstine

My story starts in 1972 as a 17-year-old married to a teenage boy-man who was a train-ride crazy pants person to live with. Our lives were insane, and by the time I hit 22, I was the divorced mother of a four-year-old boy, a high school drop-out with little prospect for a self-sustaining career other than having had worked in a dress factory up in my old hometown of Oneonta, New York and my few years of waitressing in Ocala, Florida, where I had moved to in 1975 to be closer to my parents after the breakup of a disastrous teenage marriage.

I had been waiting tables for several years, the latest of which was a little over one-year stint at the "Dragon Inn", a Chinese restaurant. The waitresses there worked twelve-hour shifts with alternating Friday nights, an erratic schedule as those types of jobs are. My parents were babysitting at the time thankfully, so that part of my life was doing okay with the exception I was exhausted from the grueling schedule and trying to keep up with a four-year-old and a work schedule that demanded fifty-to-sixty-hour weeks. The Chinese idea of a full-time work week did not fall in line with the American forty-hour work week; forty hours being looked at as a part-time position to my Chinese employers.

The waitresses in the restaurant not only waited tables, but they also served as cleaning and kitchen staff, helping to prepare food in the afternoon when business was slow and vacuuming and cleaning throughout the restaurant after closing or after the lunch rush. I learned how to make mountains of egg rolls, wontons for soup, and snip snow peas for the cooks. Those were just a small part of our duties, so by the time I got off work I was exhausted. There was a bonus, because of our long hours—we could eat rice and gravy or soup during the day and each evening after the doors were locked, and all the cleaning was done, everyone sat down for a family dinner, together. There was one caveat—you could not use flatware, chopsticks only! It didn't matter, we did it willingly. We were famished, and the food was delicious, real Chinese food. We would also eat leftover menu restaurant food that needed to be used up. Nothing ever went to waste, another Chinese trait.

I enjoyed working at the Chinese restaurant. The owners were good to me. On Chinese New Year all the employees would get a twenty-dollar bill in a red envelope for good luck. That was sweet but wouldn't do much for my retirement account or non-existent health insurance, vacation, and sick day benefits. I could take all the broken fortune cookies home I wanted for my young son, and he loved them, but it was sadly lacking in making up for no vacation or sick time. My mom and dad liked to come in for dinner occasionally and when they did, the owners made a big fuss and gave them all kinds of attention and special favors during their dinner. They did that because they were my parents, out of respect. They continued that long after I left their employ.

That said, the hours were grueling, the pay not nearly enough. I worked with an older woman in her fifties who had been a waitress all her life. She was worn out, her body wracked with pain. She was looking at a not-too-far future where she feared she couldn't continue waitressing and wasn't sure what she was going to do. She had no other training to turn to. My life was going nowhere, and glimpses of my future was reflecting back at me if I didn't take action for a different path. It seemed the solution was clear, I had to get my high school diploma, then education for a career of some sort where I could provide benefits like paid time off and health insurance for myself and my son or I was going to end up just like my older waitress friend.

I investigated the Adult Education program for Marion County and went down to their facility in early 1976. When I decided I needed to return to school, I saw no need to put it off any longer and put all my energy into it. I registered for a program where you earned actual high school credit hours for a diploma, not just take a GED test. The reasoning behind this was that I wanted to go on to the local community college for an Associate degree. I enjoyed the classes.

This program consisted of you signing up for a "class", reading the material independently and then taking a series of tests on the subject. As you passed the tests you completed the course. At the end was a final and upon passing that, you got credit for the course. After completing all required course credits Florida required, you were awarded a regular high school diploma from the Marion County School Board. I completed the 11th and 12th grades in just four months. That's a testament to the high quality of New York State's education system and my own determination to get my high school diploma quickly so I could move on to college. I had a career to get started, a child to support, and little time to accomplish it.

While I attended the Adult Education program I still worked at the Dragon Inn, working a flexible reduced hour, mostly a forty-plus hour week, a compromise by my Chinese employers.

I set my sights on enrolling in Central Florida Community College. While I was still at the Adult Education Center there was a great teacher who was an invaluable key to my success. She told me about a government program called Manpower. They paid for your tuition, books and twenty hours of class and an internship of twenty hours a week at minimum wage. This would enable me to go to school and have an income, albeit barely adequate. It was doable and a lifesaver. Without this teacher and her tip of this government program I could not have financed my college education, nor swing my full-time college attendance, and the probability of me achieving my goal would have gone down significantly.

I was accepted into the program. As a single low-income mom, I was a shoo-in. My counsellor there guided me through the process of applying and getting accepted into the local community college. My deal with Manpower was contingent on getting a timesheet signed by my college teachers each day to confirm attendance so I could be paid for attending school and I also had to keep a passing grade in each class; failure wasn't an option. I was assigned a job at the local hospital's laboratory as a receptionist late afternoons and weekends after my school hours. I quit my job at the Dragon Inn in August 1976 and entered college on August 23, 1976 and was working towards a degree in secretarial sciences. Of course, as a woman, the logical career choice for me as a single mom was that of a secretary. It sounded a lot better than waiting tables.

Beginning the transition from a waitress to student and working at the hospital laboratory was quite a change for me. The hours were still long, I put in way more than the twenty hours for school because secretarial sciences consisted of courses like English, business math and science but also business class with lab time for typing, shorthand, and office machines. I spent hours banging away at a typewriter and transcribing shorthand for a year honing my skills and speed. By this time, I had been transferred in my Manpower internship from the lab down to the Medical Records department to learn how to transcribe medical records. I was learning a new language—medical lingo. I transcribed doctor notes, admission, discharge, operative reports and many others. I was hooked on the challenge of it all. It was exciting to see how fast I could type, the words themselves, and the work of documenting medical records. It was a great job and if I was hired there were full benefits from the hospital and job stability. The manager of the department and other transcriptionists told me the field was near guaranteed to always be able to obtain a job, because the demand was high for a good medical transcriptionist. If I worked hard, studied, and did a good job at the hospital there was a good chance they would hire me after I graduated. Things were looking up.

College was hard, I attended full time taking twelve course credits each semester and even attended during the summer. I had to set time aside for extra lab hours to gain high proficiency skill at typing and shorthand. I wasn't very good at shorthand, and that meant much longer hours of practice. My teacher passed me because she said she flat out never saw anyone work so hard to learn how to do shorthand. She felt sorry for me and gave me a pass; it certainly wasn't for lack of trying. I knew how to write shorthand, I was just incapable of doing it at a speed that was at all useful regardless of how much I practiced. After uncountable hours in the lab and agonizing near tearful testing and retesting I ended up with a C and a lot of sympathy. I did better in the rest of my classes, enjoyed most of them, suffered through the ones I didn't like—science and math. I loved English and the Humanities classes, excelling at those. My grades were good, and I made the Dean's list several times.

I worked a twenty-hours/week internship at the hospital and was mom to a five-year-old boy. He began kindergarten when I began college. It was an amusing thing at the time, us starting school together. What wasn't fun was attending school and work all day, then picking my son up from mom and dad's in the evening, going home, fixing dinner or tucking him into bed and then settling down to do more schoolwork until late into the evening.

After four months of high school and twenty months of college I graduated from Central Florida Community College. At the end of the last semester, I received an invitation from the college to attend an assembly for recognition of students, but it didn't say why I'd been included, and I was baffled. There was also a note that I could invite my parents and there was a luncheon afterwards. I was hesitant to attend, because my schedule hardly allowed for extra activities such as taking time out for frivolous assemblies and luncheons, and as for inviting my parents? They were busy watching my son and I didn't think they would be interested in going to an awards assembly and luncheon with me for no clear apparent reason other than it was my graduation year.

My shorthand teacher informed me I must attend, and despite my hesitations and reservations, I did. Imagine my surprise when I was called up to the stage and then presented with the "Outstanding Student in Secretarial Sciences" award with accompanying plaque for my class. I didn't have a clue that was going to happen. My teacher had pressed for my receiving of the class award. She knew how hard I worked and what obstacles had been in my path, and that despite them all I had persevered and exceeded expectations.

The next surprise that happened was I got a notification that Phi Theta Kappa was inducting me into their ranks because of my outstanding academic performance. I had managed to place on the Dean's List twice and had a very high B+ to A average overall. I missed graduating with honors by .1, enough for me to have lost sleep in disappointment, but in retrospect still an accomplishment. At the time of my May 2, 1978 graduation, I was twenty-four years old and had completed two years of high school and an associate degree in Medical Secretarial Sciences at Central Florida Community College within twenty-four months.

My internship turned into a real job offer when the hospital hired me full-time and I obtained my dream—a full-time job at a wage I could live on working a forty-hour week, complete with a full benefit package; vacation, sick time, health insurance and a retirement package to boot! I had transformed my life in two years from a dead-end job to what turned out to be a life career with recession-proof job security.

It all had become a reality with the help of a teacher who cared at a local Adult Education Center and with a government program for low-income single moms, where if you were willing to work for it, you could get an education and a new career in order to become an asset to society and not a burden, have a chance to start a new life for yourself, and perhaps accomplish a dream.

In the end I want to thank my teacher from the Adult Education Center all those years ago. She really kept me on track in school and then made sure I had a way to pay for college and pay my bills while attending school full-time. The people at Manpower were awesome and deserve a big thank you. The program covered all the costs of going to school so I could just focus on my education and work experience. The government doesn't always get things right, but that was a great program and sure changed my life for the better.

ℰ☯ℂ☮

Lost in Translation
By Patricia Daly-Lipe

After spending over two years in Europe, I returned to Washington, D.C. My first job was at the *Evening Star* newspaper. I was to answer the incoming calls from reporters on the scene. The "scene" could be a murder, a robbery, an accident, a fire. It was always something traumatic.

After listening to the reporter, I was to write his/her report and submit the article for the newspaper. Unfortunately, I could not understand what the reporters were saying most of the time. They were speaking so quickly. But why not? They were in a horrendous situation! But repeat? No, they did not want or have time to repeat.

Why did I not understand? I had been speaking French and Italian for almost three years. These reporters had southern accents. Of course, English is my native tongue, but my ear for their accent was not in tune. So, the paper placed me in a new position: Writing obituaries.

I have always loved meeting and speaking with people and hearing their stories, so, in my new position, my day-to-day experience allowed me to meet people I never would have known before. Many of my stories related to the passing of African Americans, and with Washington still being segregated, honoring the lives of the deceased in a tribute, mattered a lot to some wonderful and compassionate people and I am grateful for that experience. To this day, my philosophy stems from my first job, and is evidenced in many of my books.

Notes for your memories of this age:

I MATTER TOO!

CHAPTER 4

The Age of Action:
Work / Career

ᴓᴖ

A Magic Moment
By Harlan Rector

In 1946, at age 12 with $5 in my pocket, I'd take a bus and streetcar to north St. Louis and spend an entire Saturday at Don Lawton's Magic Den. In wonder, I watched local magicians come in the store to see what new tricks he had up his sleeve.

Fast forward 24 years to 1970. While I was an art director in the largest advertising agency in Detroit, a copywriter, Larry, and I were sent to Los Angeles to meet a client in preparation for creating an advertising campaign.

Our very first trip to LA promised to be a real treat since Larry had a friend, a young actor named Fred, who promised to pick us up at the airport and give us a grand tour. As we were driving through Beverly Hills, Fred suddenly said, "Hey, how would you guys like to visit the Magic Castle in Hollywood?" The word Magic got my attention, so I said, "What's in the Magic Castle?" Fred continues, "It's a private club where magicians from all over the world gather to entertain the members and their guests." Just the thought of it brought magic tricks floating about in my head like candy and toys to a boy at Christmas.

We drove up in the hills of Hollywood to the entrance of a gorgeous castle, valet parked and entered the lobby. The interior of the Castle reception was every bit as castle-like as the exterior. A very nice receptionist greets us, "Good evening, gentlemen, how may I help you?" Fred steps up and says, "Yes, I'm from NBC here in LA and these men are from NBC in New York and I'd like to show them around." "This is a private club, are you a member?" "No, but we're with NBC, I'm sure they have a membership we could…" She interrupts, "I'm sorry, I can't let you enter."

Fred tried another approach to no avail so we turned and headed for the door. She continues, "…unless you can do a magic trick for me." Without hesitation, I reached into my pocket for a quarter and approached the reception desk. My two friends stop at the door wide-eyed. I show the coin between two fingers in one hand, pretend to pass it to the other hand, snap my fingers and the quarter disappears to show both hands empty, the finger snap shooting the coin up the sleeve of my sport coat. The receptionist smiles and says, "That's the smoothest finger snap I've ever seen."

My two friends are speechless. I can let you enter if a member will vouch for you. Do you know a member or a performing magician?" I said, "The only magician I know is Don Lawton in St. Louis. I used to buy my magic tricks at his store." The receptionist says, "Don Lawton?" I nodded. "He's here tonight", she said. I almost fainted. "What's your name, sir?" she asked. She dials a number and said, "Mr. Lawton, there's a gentleman here who is asking you to vouch for him. His name is Harlan Rector. He knows you from St. Louis." She hangs up saying, "Mr. Lawton will be right down." We hadn't seen each other in 24 years, so when he came in I shook his hand and said, "When I was a kid I used to…"

Don interrupted me and said, "Are you that kid who used to hang around all day to spend five dollars?" I nodded and Don told the three of us to turn around and face this huge bookcase. Don whispered, "Say this magic word I'm going to tell you". I said the magic word and the whole bookcase swiveled open to reveal a magnificent, ornate bar. People sitting there turned to see who the next visitor might be. I'd tell you that magic word, but a good magician never reveals how a trick is done. Don ushered us in to a "magical" evening I'll never forget.

The Magic Castle is on several levels with large and small theatres where magic is performed non-stop. There are several close-up areas where four or five guests sit across a small table from the magician in a semi-circle. Most are card tricks, coin tricks, the balls and cups, anything that can be viewed up-close. Everyone is happily amazed.

In one room there is a grand piano, with a name that escapes me. I'll call the piano "Bessie". People sit in the room and say, "Bessie, play Alexander's Ragtime Band or Moon River or Beethoven's Fifth." The keys start playing by themselves and Bessie will even respond, musically, to your conversation. Such fun. Upstairs is a wonderful dining room with fabulous food and service. If you dine there you will be first in line at any of the theatres for the next scheduled shows.

I visited the Magic Castle every time I had a trip to LA. Our family moved to Los Angeles in 1975 and I've taken everyone to the Castle so they can experience the fun of being bewildered. Magicians come from all over the country, Europe and the Far East as guest performers.

I'm not sure magic, like singing, dancing or performing anything is life-changing for an audience, but it sure is entertaining and, for the most part, a positive influence for everyone, especially the performer.

ℰℭ

What Goes Into the First of Life
By Jenny L. Cote

My first memory of life is standing in the middle of the road, clad only in a diaper, holding up traffic. I had slipped out of the house and gone on walkabout with our dog, Tip. My brother was shouting for me to get out of the street before he ran inside to tell my mother who was teaching a piano lesson. Meanwhile, I stood there staring down a grey Chevy, fearless in my cloth diaper and pins. The blood drained from my mother's face when she saw what her toddler was doing, and she promptly ran outside to retrieve me. She must have felt her dreams of receiving the Mother-of-the-Year award slipping through her toddler-gripped fingers.

I haven't changed much.

The diaper-in-the-road moment has led to similar situations throughout life. I've given my parents more than a few frights, like climbing so high up the mast to the crow's nest of our sailboat that I couldn't get down. Or jumping overboard to snorkel alone in the Bahamas to face three barracudas by myself. Or taking the wave-runner out so far in the ocean that my dad thought I was shark bait. There was the incident where I accidentally set off the alarm at Patrick Henry's house in Virginia, with two sheriff's deputies pulling guns on me. And being kicked out of the Mamertine Prison in Rome so I could research a little longer. My carpe diem sense of adventure has gotten me into trouble, but it has also gotten me into good.

Little did I know that when I was a toddler roaming the battlefields of Yorktown, or a child skipping down Duke of Gloucester Street in Williamsburg that I would someday write America's story as a children's historical fiction author. Nor did I know that as I wrote stories of talking fruit as an eight-year-old that I would write stories of talking animals as an adult. Or when I boldly went selling my books door to door for a dime that I would someday be selling books around the globe as I speak to kids about my adventures in researching and writing. I've shared with kids that I sat in George F. Handel's composing room in London to write the scene of him writing the Messiah. And I spent two nights in C.S. Lewis's house and interviewed his secretary in the Eagle and Child pub in Oxford because I asked boldly and seized the day when they said "yes." I tell kids to pursue their wildest dreams and ask big for things, because they are loved, and they are able to achieve more than they could ever hope for or imagine.

I know I was born wired for adventure—it's in my DNA. I've always been this way. But the primary reason I've pulled off all of this crazy stuff is because of what was first instilled in me as a child by my parents. I was loved unconditionally, raised in a home filled with joy and safety, and taught to love Jesus and my country. My parents didn't have a lot of earthly wealth to give me, but what they gave me was worth more than any fading trinket or possession. They gave me a rock-solid foundation of unshakable self-confidence to go out and conquer my world with my God-given skills and passions. They broadened my horizons with experiences rich in history, learning and adventure. And yes, they disciplined me so I would learn respect for authority and rules, and so I would treat others with courtesy.

When a child feels safe, loved, encouraged, and is taught to follow God and the Golden Rule, they have a solid foundation on which to build a life. When the storms come, that child will be able to weather it well and come out stronger as a result. My parents knew this, for their stormy childhoods were undergirded by amazing, godly mothers despite their harmful fathers. They were determined that the painful things they experienced as children would not be repeated in our home, and they weren't. Perhaps it was my grandmother's oft-repeated phrase that drove home their resolve: "What goes into the first of life goes throughout all of life."

Think of that. What goes into the first of life goes throughout all of life. Joy, pain, happiness, fear, goodness, evil, adventure, sadness, calm or rage. Whatever a child experiences will follow them throughout all of life. If goodness is poured into them, it will pour out of them. If badness is poured into them, badness will pour out of them—unless a counter-balance is given to help them cope and overcome. Reflect on your own life, and you will see this is true. Does that mean that if you experienced a childhood of badness, your future will also be filled with badness? Not necessarily. It depends on how you choose to respond to your "first of life" moments.

If you want to have a different future than your past, change it. Give it all to Jesus – your past, present and future, and He will redeem every moment of it for your highest good. "For I know the plans I have for you," declares the Lord, "plans to prosper you and not to harm you, plans to give you hope and a future (Jeremiah 29:11)." Someone once said that Christianity is the only religion that deals with a person's past. Only God could bring good from bad, both for the individual and for the world.

Because I was raised to extend the tenderness and love of God to others, I'm passionate about giving special attention to a hurting child. I recently received this note from a young woman:

> About ten years ago, you visited my middle school to talk about your career in creative writing. You talked about the research process and how much you loved it and how essential it is in your field. Hearing you speak made me believe that I could also one day become a writer, which is why I am reaching out to you today.
>
> Trying to figure out my voice, tap deep into my imagination, and the research process have become extremely overwhelming. I can feel my thoughts and my stories conforming to how others will perceive them rather than actually getting my vision down on paper. I'm unable to become the best storyteller I can be due to the fear of rejection and criticism. I am reaching out to see if I could ask you for some advice? Your resume is incredible and I have no right to ask you for help especially when you're busy with the fictional universe you have created.
>
> If you don't respond, I understand completely and apologize for wasting your time. Thank you so much for taking the time to read this message.

Did you read between the lines? Do you see her lack of self-confidence and her low self-worth? I can only assume that what went into the first of her life was negativity, and it is now plaguing her as she tries to chart her course and pursue her dream to be a writer. It gripped my heart and I immediately responded that I am honored to have inspired her and am overjoyed to help her in her quest. Never underestimate the impact you will have on a child.

What goes into the first of life goes throughout all of life. Be careful, then, how you treat the next generation. Fill them with love and high self-esteem. Fill them with joy and goodness. And fill them with the hope of a life lived pursuing God. And all of life will be worth living.

ଏଠଓ

Timing and Talent Matters
By Greg Barry

When I look back at the important decisions I've made in my life, it's amazing to think about how many times they've been influenced by luck and timing. Those elements have affected many of my decisions when it came to things like the college I chose, jobs I've accepted, and even involving the woman who agreed to marry me.

At one point in my career, I worked with a colleague named Ann. We were peers and occasionally worked on projects together. She'd been working at the company for a while and over time we'd had a few personal conversations. She was born and raised in the Twin Cities, where we were based, and she had attended a local university.

She shared a situation from early in her career when she'd accepted a job in Chicago. It was a good job in a well-established organization and she knew she had the skills necessary to succeed.

So, she relocated. It was a fresh start, a new beginning, working in a major city with many resources available to a young professional.

Ann attended her first day at work which included a two-week orientation. At the end of the first week Ann resigned, nervously informing her supervisor that it just wasn't going to work out. Her supervisor was confused as she expected Ann would be a good fit for the position.

Ann apologized. She knew she was letting her new supervisor down, and she was also letting herself down.

She moved back to the Twin Cities and took a job at a local company where she felt safe and secure.

Several years later, she began working at my company. It didn't take long for her to establish herself as a hard worker, a team player and as a pleasant person. I noticed one day she didn't seem her usual ebullient self. She told me she was having a rough week and was feeling a little down.

She then asked me if I had a few minutes to speak privately. She told me that a few weeks prior, Microsoft had reached out to her through her Linked-In page asking if she was interested in applying for a job with them. She contacted them and had had two phone interviews. They then flew her to Seattle for a panel interview.

Microsoft contacted her offering her the job the next Monday. After thinking long and hard about what to do, she decided to call them back to decline the position and it had now been 48 hours since she'd made that fateful call.

She told me it would have been a great opportunity but things were going well at home and she liked being close to her family and old friends.

I asked if her decision had anything to do with the Chicago situation when she was fresh out of college. After a long pause, she admitted her decision had a lot to do with that unfortunate experience. She had failed before and didn't want it to happen again. She believed people in her life would think less of her if she failed again. She said the debacle in Chicago took a long time to recover from and she didn't want to take the risk of it happening again.

She hadn't asked me for advice but since she was sharing her troubling situation with me, I felt I should offer some perspective. I asked if the position was a good opportunity to which she answered "yes". I asked if they offered a generous benefits package, she said "yes" and that she would be earning four weeks of vacation time annually. I responded, "so that's plenty of time to visit friends and family each year." And, I added, "anyone who thinks less of you if you come home again probably isn't worth your time and energy anyway."

She agreed with a smile, saying she wouldn't have interviewed if she didn't think it could work out. She added she didn't think she would even receive an offer. She told me she had probably blown it by already turning down the position. I suggested that if she had a renewed interest in the position, it wouldn't hurt to call to ask if she could still accept their offer.

She was sure the position had already been offered to another candidate. She asked aloud, "what idiot would turn down a job at Microsoft?" She grinned slightly and thanked me for listening and for the reality check.

The next morning, she came bounding into my office with great news. She had called Microsoft asking if the position was still open. They transferred the call to the hiring manager who re-offered the position to Ann.

As an afterthought, she said she thought I was supposed to have been on vacation that week. I told her she was right but that I'd postponed it until the following week. "Lucky me," she responded.

Ann's success at Microsoft has had everything to do with her skills, abilities, and talent level. She was right for the position and the organization. Microsoft is lucky to have her. My small involvement in the process had only to do with luck and timing. The nudge just happened to come at the right time.

Ann has been with Microsoft for 10 years now and has received several promotions since she started. She is raising two daughters with her husband and they are very happy living in the upper northwest.

I receive a Christmas card from her every year. I'm glad things worked out well for her. She deserves it.

୫)ଔ

A Dream Come True
By Jeff Rector

Growing up in Bloomfield Hills, Michigan, I loved to watch old black and white films, especially cheesy horror and science fiction films. The horror films that made the biggest impression on me were the Universal Pictures classic monster movies with Bela Lugosi as Count Dracula, Boris Karloff as Frankenstein and Lon Chaney, Jr. as The Wolfman.

Universal would later take a big chance and merge two of their biggest box office properties, the comedy duo of Bud Abbott and Lou Costello, and combine them with their famous monsters into a comedy/horror mash-up called *Abbott & Costello Meet Frankenstein*.

This was a huge leap of faith for Universal for if it failed, it would forever damage the image of their famous monsters by making them look silly alongside two vaudevillian comedians. But it worked. *Abbott and Costello Meet Frankenstein* was a box-office hit! What I love most about the film is that the original actors playing the monsters played their parts deadly serious as though it was a true horror film. That made the monsters believable and added the major drama juxtaposed to the comedy relief, Abbott and Costello.

Science fiction films were produced in much greater numbers since they were much cheaper to produce. Sci-fi "B" movies played on television every week. Titles like *Tarantula, The Brain from Planet Arous, The Mole People, Revenge of the Creature* (the sequel to the *Creature From The Black Lagoon*), and many others. What did all these sci-fi films have in common? They all starred actor John Agar.

John's career started with big budget westerns at the time of *Fort Apache* starring with John Wayne, Henry Fonda and Shirley Temple (who he would marry many years later) and *She Wore A Yellow Ribbon*. Later that year, John would re-team with John Wayne in the World War II drama *The Sands of Iwo Jima*, their third film together in three years.

I knew John from Saturday afternoon sci-fi films like *Attack of the Puppet People, The Daughter of Dr. Jekyll* and an episode of the *The Twilight Zone*. I'd watch John Agar starring in all these films and think, "What a handsome leading man, always kissing the beautiful leading ladies. If I were an actor, I'd want to be like John Agar." But I was just a 13-year-old kid living in the Midwest. I might as well want to be an astronaut; that would be just as likely to happen.

My father, Harlan Rector, worked in advertising and in 1975, the family moved west to Tarzana in the San Fernando Valley, outside Los Angeles, California. It was named Tarzana after the famous author Edgar Rice Burroughs who created and wrote the iconic "Tarzan" novels about the "King of the Apes" who lived there at the time. Burroughs named his daughter Tara and his son Zan.

Shortly after moving to Tarzana, our father took us to the Universal Studios Tour in Universal City. I couldn't believe it, the actual studio that made some of my favorite monster movies! I would quickly realize that the Universal Studios Tour was completely separate from the actual Universal Pictures Studio. The tour showed us (and a tram full of other tourists) the secrets and magic of how movies are made.

I was instantly smitten and decided that I wanted to be a Universal Tour Guide. The reality was that everyone wanted to be a Universal Tour Guide. 3,000 applicants/year would try to get into the training program with only 30 openings.

I applied and miraculously, I got selected for the arduous training, having to memorize over two and a half hours of studio information that we had to verbally share on every tour. It was pretty grueling in the summer outside in the 95 -104 degree heat.

We were also paid minimum wage of $2.47/hour. Every Tour Guide that was hired had big Hollywood dreams of being discovered by Universal Studios and getting an acting contract. We all learned rather quickly that was not the case, we were just minimum wage Amusement Park employees.

Flash forward ten years. I had an agent, a manager and I was guest-starring on such TV show as *Father Dowling Mysteries* opposite Tom Bosley (Mr. Cunningham on *Happy Days*), *Star Trek: The Next Generation*, opposite Patrick Stewart, and *NYPD Blue* opposite Dennis Franz and Jimmy Smits, plus many other popular shows at the time. Over the years, I've worked for all the major studios, but since my early years working as a Tour Guide, I've always felt that Universal Studios was my home studio, especially because of my early love for the Universal monsters.

Because of *Star Trek: TNG*, I got into a lot of science fiction conventions all over the world signing autographs and assorted memorabilia from various shows I'd worked on. At the time, there was an annual autograph show in North Hollywood at the Beverly Garland Hotel. Beverly Garland was a famous actress who also starred in a lot "B" sci-fi films like *Swamp Women, The Alligator People* and *It Conquered the World*. Beverly bought the North Hollywood Holiday Inn and she turned it into the Beverly Garland Hotel, completely remodeling it, adorning the inside with her pictures and memorabilia from her career in television and motion pictures.

I was invited on several occasions to be a celebrity guest and signed autographs with everyone from Don Knotts (Barney Fife from *The Andy Griffith Show*) to Linda Blair (*The Exorcist*). So I'm running late for the show which has already started. I rush to my autograph table. I reach into my bag and start throwing my headshots and photographs down onto my table. I quickly organize everything the best I can and then sit down and take a deep breath and sigh of relief. I take a moment to take in the room to see what other celebrities are there that day.

I look around and sitting at the table right next to me is JOHN AGAR! I was completely taken aback. John was 80 years old, but still looked great. He looked over at all my pictures and said, "You've done a lot of work!" I looked at him and said, "Oh my gosh! You're John Agar!" He smiled held out his hand and said, "What's your name?" I shook his hand, gushed, and said, "Jeff Rector". He said, "Nice to meet you, Jeff!"

In that moment, all of those memories of *Tarantula*, *The Mole People* and *The Brain from Planet Arous* came flooding back. I said, "I have to tell you, John, I grew up watching your movies as a kid and I said to myself, 'John Agar, what a handsome leading man, if I was ever was an actor, that's who I'd want to be.'" John blushed a little and said. "Why thank you, Jeff!" I continued on, "You're the person that inspired me! I grew up in Michigan. The last thing you think about is being a movie star, but you inspired me and that wasn't even my dream at the time. And now I'm a leading man in TV and film. And that's all because you inspired me at age 13!"

At this point, I see John's demeanor instantly change. His whole face lights up and he gets a huge smile on his face. "Well thank you, Jeff, that's about the nicest thing anyone's ever said to me!" "You're welcome!" I said. "It's a real pleasure!" I could see in his eyes that that was an incredible "wow moment" for both of us, that he actually inspired a complete stranger who would become successful and actually meet each other twenty-nine years later.

Then some people came over to our tables. I signed some pictures from Star Trek and John signed some pictures from *The Sands of Iwo Jima* where he's in an action pose alongside John Wayne. I never saw

John Agar again and I read in the *Hollywood Reporter* that he passed away shortly afterwards in 2002, leaving behind a great body of work as his legacy. In that special moment between us, John Agar knew that he mattered.

Today, in addition to acting and directing and producing my own films, I enjoy teaching acting workshops and shepherding a whole new generation of actors toward a successful career. We all matter in one way or another and I continue to use my celebrity to give back as much as possible and to support worthwhile charities and humanitarian causes around the world.

✧❀✧

Pray for the Sudanese
By Chuck Brockmeyer

March 7, 2002:

I was in early morning prayer as was my habit. I was trying to hear from God instead of just me asking for all my needs, hopes and worries as usual. I had heard about a new way of praying, being quiet before God. I was doing this when I had a vision of a large and wide torrent of a river coming from the throne of God. I believed it was the loving actions of God, giving life, saving lives, healing the sick, blessing, giving kindness to the oppressed, multifold wisdom, consultations, compassion, benefits upon benefits. The river never stopped and I thought if I just dipped my hand into it I would be able to feel God's work. Then, in the stillness, words, or a thought, or something inside me says "Pray for Sudan."

"Oh, pray for Sudan, OK", I thought to myself, "sounds good, I will pray for the Sudanese Christians." I had heard terrible stories about the great persecution of Christians ongoing in that country and the almost complete silence about it in America, so I started a focused effort to pray for them.

That same morning I jump into the car ready to drive to work. I turn on the radio and the first thing it says was, "March for Sudan at the state capital this Saturday being held to bring awareness to the plight of the persecuted people living there. Approximately 2 million people have been killed in the last 17 years in an ongoing civil war."

I can't believe what I'm hearing on the radio. It really sounds like confirmation to me to get involved. So, I made up my mind to get to the capital that day and attend the event. I told my wife about all that happened and took off for the capital. I arrived early and had time to tour the inside of the capital itself. Around all of the walls in one wing of the capital were 50 or so very inspiring statements, all made by patriots and leaders of our country. Their faith in God and their resolve to preserve freedom and respect for all men made you wonder how all of this separation of church and state came into being especially when these early fathers of our country had such solid faith in God and voiced it eloquently!

Back outside, the Sudan event was taking place. It was an eye-opening experience with many personal stories of escape, murders of family members, torture and courage of a people undergoing inhuman religious cleansing. I sensed there was someone in the crowd I knew and before long a fellow Christian from our evangelism committee was standing beside me saying how they also had been led to come to this event. Cool, I thought. The whole day was very moving and I made up my mind to do something, but what?

A few days later, the phone rings and a woman says, "Hello, are you the pastor who was interested in having me speak at your church about the plight of the persecuted Sudanese Christians?"

Totally surprised I replied, "No, no I wasn't, not a pastor, but yes, that's a great idea. I will certainly talk to the pastor to see if we can have you come and speak. But sorry, who are you?"

She replied "I am Dr. Pat, the one who hosted the March for Sudan at the Capital last Saturday!"

Wow, how did she get my name? I must have put my name and number down on some roster during the event. She went on to explain that she was in full time mission work, had been trained under Brother Andrew (who wrote the book, *God's Smuggler*) and was heavily involved in encouraging and bringing Bibles to churches in countries where Christians are persecuted.

We had a good conversation and soon afterward our Church invited Dr. Pat to Zion's Adult Forum where she gave a sobering presentation on the holocaust in Sudan. That Sunday and another Sunday afterward I saw a Sudanese family at our church—then they disappeared and didn't come back again. This disturbed me and I thought, "How can we reach out to the local Sudanese?" No ideas came to me.

About a year and a half later, it was Missions Sunday. Pastor Cherian of AGORA Ministries was invited to give a sermon at our church, Zion, and his message was inspiring and admonishing.

Pastor Cherian started out, "The church of Jesus Christ belongs to all Christians it is not just a club where people come to be members." You can imagine how the rest of his sermon went. He talked about all the refugees, aliens and other countries present in our local area and why aren't they here with us?

Hearing his words affected me deeply and I remembered how I wanted to reach out to the Sudanese a year and a half ago. A couple of days later I decided to call AGORA Ministries hoping to get some advice from Pastor Cherian on how to find the local Sudanese, since for me they seemed to be invisible.

I picked up the phone and dialed the number. Pastor Cherian answered the phone, and so I began my question, "Hello, I just wanted to call about the Sudanese in our area…"

Pastor Cherian broke in before I could finish my sentence, "Are you the pastor from Zion I talked to that wanted to meet with the Sudanese Community leaders?"

I said, "No, no, I am not. I mean I'm not a pastor, but that is what I have in my heart to do, and was calling just now to see how I can help."

He immediately replied, "Well, I am glad you asked. I have some of the Sudanese community leaders that want to meet with your church and talk about joining with you. They would like to do this on Sunday at 5:00 p.m. Can you set it up?"

"I certainly will try!" was my reply.

And POW! There we were Sunday at 5:00 p.m. with nine Sudanese elders, our pastoral staff and Pastor Cherian. The Sudanese were comprised of a spiritual leader, Mawien Ariik, a community leader, Clements, three or four women, an elder, and a young man who interpreted for the elder. The main elder explains that they have no permanent place to hold worship services and would like to request holding them at our church.

I listen intently to what is being discussed and find out that there are about 150 Sudanese in the area plus many others scattered around some bordering states.

It appears all is going well with the discussion and the pastoral staff at Zion are all in for this new relationship—behind it 100%. The timing seemed to be perfect. Another meeting later and the first worship time is planned. The week after that 70 or so Sudanese gathered for worship in the small chapel of our church. They brought along their African music, beautiful singing and a great sermon in both Arabic and English. The sermon went something like this, with Mawien speaking, "We were in a small boat on a great and troubled sea when we came to the USA. Then Zion invited us to come to a safe harbor and the sea and wind were immediately quiet. Our Bible says only God can command the sea and wind to be quiet! We are here because of Jesus Christ!"

I couldn't believe how quickly it all came together. I agreed with Mawien; it had to be God.

The planned joining of the Sudanese Church with ours got a lot of attention from some of the higher-up positions in the church. At the first Sudanese service an assistant to the bishop of the Minneapolis Synod was there along with a pastor from the big Lutheran Church, Central Lutheran, in downtown Minneapolis. The event was printed up with photos in AGORA Mission's newsletter the following week.

Now, four services later, our church has created a task force of ten people to handle the issues and needs of this new relationship as well as a suggestion for a new chair position to Zion's council called the Cultural Diversity Chair.

A few years after these events, Mawien, the Sudanese spiritual leader, was sponsored at a Theological college to become a full-fledged Lutheran Pastor. Besides Zion he covers five Sudanese Churches in a five-state area. He has also gone back to Sudan to the area where his father's tribe lives and baptized 70 people and planted five seed churches. Now in 2008 he is on second trip back to Sudan checking the progress of his first visit and carrying with him $5,000 of donations that will be enough funds to build one church building.

It just goes to show you, when you connect with God's heart on a matter you will see his hand move in a mighty way—and the best thing about it is, you get to be involved yourself!

৪০০৪

The Chinese/English Bibles
By Chuck Brockmeyer

A big question being asked in modern society today is "Is the Bible God's own inspired words or just a concoction of man, used in manipulating and controlling people to obey an outdated set of rules?" The questions I would ask is, "Would God work to promote the spread of the Bible by miracles if it were not His own words? And what is it He is trying to tell us?"

I was doing an engineering study at an edible oil facility in Liaoyang N. E. China and would be there for about a week. As I sat alone in an office behind a long, long conference table, working away on my project, I wondered how I was going to get Internet service. A Chinese fellow entered the room and introduced himself to me, "Hello, I'm Mr. Gary Hu, you can call me Mr. Gary. I'm a friend of the owner of the plant. I do some broker work for Mr. Li, supplying him with soybeans from Ohio, USA. I don't charge him anything because we are strictly friends."

Mr. Gary, a Chinese-American, looked familiar. He was a very helpful fellow, going out of his way to be friendly to me, letting me use his Internet connection, giving me advice about life in China. Gary seemed to be an interesting and charismatic character that had great business savvy plus a lot of connections in China. He was a welcome presence in a place where I didn't speak the language and had no contacts.

Back in my hotel room, trying to get comfortable with the two blankets on plywood board instead of a mattress, my mind drifted back to how I ended up in China. Our oil seed department's vice president, Chris Heeb, entered my cubicle and said he would like me to get prepared for a trip to China. He would like me to fly to Liaoyang Edible Oil Company and do an engineering study of how to install a new soybean dehulling system in the existing plant structure.

In getting ready for the trip I had come up with the idea to contact Dr. Pat and see if there was anything I could do to help her in her work with persecuted Christian groups in China. She worked with the famous Father Andrew who wrote the book *God's Smuggler*, which was filled with amazing stories of passing suitcases full of Bibles right under the eyes of customs agents as though God blinded them to what they were really seeing! She had told me she did her ministry in countries where Christian missionary work was forbidden. She went by the name Dr. Pat due to terroristic threats and possible retribution.

I remembered attending The March for Sudan at the Minnesota Capital and how, in meeting Dr. Pat, she had started the ball rolling on getting a place of worship for the Sudanese refugees in our church in Anoka, Minnesota.

Then I recalled how great God works as I responded to a nagging urgency to call Dr. Pat right away before I left on my business trip. Even though it was late in the evening, I called. It had been perfect timing. When she picked up the phone there was the noise of packing going on in the background. She told me if I had called her the next day she would have been long gone. When I asked her about China she said she had nothing going on in China at this time but I should contact a Mr. J at International Bible Givers and see if he had any Chinese translations that they would like distributed in China. I called him the very next day. To my disappointment, Mr. J stated he had no translations available, but then after thinking a moment he said another contact he knew might have something for me. It was a day before my trip and I was ready to give up when there, on the doorstep, were two Chinese/English Bible translations with a note that said he would pray they got into the right hands. Great.

Then there was the question: I had my Bibles, now to whom was I going to give them? Dr. Pat would have said, "Just believe in God to arrange everything. God is the one in control." I prayed, "God, please organize for someone who needs these Bibles to meet me in China." And feeling like "that was that", my faith was fixed and I was ready for a long trip to China!

Now back to reality, I was back at the jobsite: Very tough work to complete in China, very poor working and living conditions. No heat in the hotel or facility and in the plant there were just a few single light bulbs hanging from the ceiling, but I saw God helping me at every turn. Even with the primitive environment I felt that the trip is going to go well. The interpreter, Mr. Song, was given me by our Beijing office and he turned out to be much more than just an interpreter. He arranged travel, got drivers, called taxis, bickered and dealt to get my expenses taken care of with the customer. Over dinner, he would give me numerous insights into Chinese life.

But even with all the extra help I was getting pretty exhausted, feeling lonely and in need of some English conversation. You know how the maintenance manual of some rechargeable battery-operated devices says to let the battery run down completely before recharging because this helps them maintain full capacity. Similarly, I felt so low I asked God if he was running me down to "empty" so he could get full capacity out of me later.

I finished up with the study and did some sketches for the head engineer. The customer was satisfied with the work and wished Mr. Song and me a good trip back to the States. A driver was called to transport several people, and just by chance Mr. Gary Hu, to the airport where we would end up in Beijing for a night at the hotel before leaving the country. Traveling along, Mr. Gary was an avid conversationalist, changing effortlessly from Chinese to English and back again as he conversed with the Chinese in the back seat and then with me in the front. He talked about his commodities brokering business in China and his home in New York and his past work with the United Nations.

Mr. Gary knew I was spending the night in a hotel in Beijing, as was he, in fact he was staying in a hotel nearby. He invited me to have supper with him, stating that he had been born in Beijing and would show me around the city. I hesitantly agreed even though I was completely worn out from several long days and nights at the job site and wanted nothing more than to hit the sack.

In the hotel room, getting ready for dinner, I flopped on the bed and I wondered out loud, "Here I am, the trip is almost over and nothing has come up concerning those Bibles. No one has approached me; I can't speak Chinese or take time to locate any underground Christian churches. God, are you going to bring someone to me for these books?"

As soon as the words left my mouth a vision flashed into my mind; the Bibles I had with the English text and Chinese text and then Mr. Gary, both an American and a Chinese. Hmm. I had to wonder, is Mr. Gary Hu the one? I prayed right then and there, saying to God, "Mr.

Gary will have to say something to me as a signal, then I would know it is You leading me and not my own imagination."

Mr. Gary picked me up and we drove into the city to a very nice French restaurant and amazingly enough had Cajun Etouffee, the classic Louisiana stew. We ate on the second story outside deck looking out at lights and colors of Beijing's looming skyscrapers that could rival any in New York City.

As we talked Mr. Gary explained both he and our client came from backgrounds of terrible poverty. Mr. Li, the owner of the oil seed facility, as a boy, was abused and beaten nearly every day by his father — mainly because he was sickly and couldn't bring in much money to help the family. Then one day Mr. Li took a bundle of rice from the country into the city to see if he could sell it at a profit. He could and he did. This was the very start of his successful business career and as he continued to sell and trade he became more and more fruitful. After a time Mr. Li fell into a "once in a lifetime" opportunity with the Chinese government. A government-run soybean-processing plant could not turn a profit and was going bankrupt. This plant was practically given to Mr. Li, along with all the machinery. He turned the company into a success and started a new, more modern company in Liaoyang and expanded into real estate.

Mr. Gary said everything Mr. Li touched turned to gold. Now Li was worth millions, but his father was still abusing him, barging into his office, throwing around furniture and demanding, "Your money is my money! Give me my money!" Then Mr. Gary said something that gave me a shot of electricity. He said, "Being a Christian man, I told Mr. Li, 'When your father doesn't like you, you need to have Jesus! God likes you and will make you feel better!'" Gary told me he always tells Mr. Li he needs Jesus, but this hadn't turned him into a Christian yet.

Ah! This was the signal I had been waiting for! I reached over and shook his hand saying, "Hey! We are brothers then, I'm a fellow believer."

With that statement, we began a great and interesting conversation, which included a story of Mr. Gary's life and how he became a Christian. Here's a summary of his conversion:

As a boy in Beijing, his father had been involved in the Cultural Revolution but was arrested and died in prison, leaving young Gary and his mother in abject poverty. The boys at school didn't like him, saying he was of the wrong family. Even so he continued to study very hard and get good grades, saying, "I wanted to try to make everything perfect." Then a milestone event happened for him; there was a national testing of Chinese students for college entrance scholarships. He took the test and was ranked second highest in all the testing! Now his college education was secure and with hard work he received a master's degree in physics. Again, a one of a kind opportunity came his way; more testing for a United Nations position, which he entered. He was accepted as department head of the Science and Education Department for the U.N.

The next step in his life, Mr. Gary was given a career with the Prime Minister of Beijing, scheduling all meetings for the provincial governors of China and their meetings at the Parliament Building. Gary really felt he had found his dream when disaster struck. He took part in the Tiananmen Square demonstration, which ended both his career and the Prime Minister's. The Prime Minister was a huge advocate of the demonstrations, but now was told to step down. Gary didn't fare too well either and was exiled to the USA with only $100 in his pocket. So again poverty stricken, he entered the United States as a political refugee. But here his life would change.

All the exiles were welcomed with open arms into the U.S. With only a small amount of cash in his pocket he hoped for some financial support but found none, until a Christian couple came forward and offered him a place to stay in Ohio. This Ohio couple was instrumental in bringing Gary, the life-long atheist, to the Lord. Mr. Gary said they helped him on his path to belief by showing him hospitality, bringing him to their church every Sunday, giving him a Bible and telling him his need for Jesus Christ.

Mr. Gary was brought up in the communist mindset, that there is no God, but now, Gary would say to himself, "God could be real. I'm going to check it out." He would read the Bible and listen at church, but would come up with many unanswered questions. In fact the couple he lived with was becoming exhausted by all the questions, some for which they had no answers. Finally his Christian sponsors brought him in to discuss these things with a panel of Catholic priests. Gary asked them many questions.

At the question, "Why does an all-powerful God allow all this shame and hurt in the world?" a priest, frustrated with all his questions, finally told him, "Why don't you ask God why and see what he says?" Gary thought, "Yes, I will ask God directly."

So, that night Gary, very seriously, asked, "God if you're real, tell me." And to his surprise his answer was clearly and simply given and God did so in such a way that Gary "knew that he knew" that He, God, was the Truth, and the Life. From that day on Gary was totally confident in his belief in Jesus Christ and His love for him. He doubled down on his studying of the Bible, tried to tell others they need Jesus and later after moving to New York, established a small home church meeting at his apartment.

I told him, "Your story is really inspiring, I bet your enthusiasm has led many people to Christ."

He answered, "Yes, I have and that's why they now call me Happy Gary!" That night we had a great Christian talk as we drove by Tiananmen Square, the Chinese Parliament and the Forbidden City, where surprisingly The Three Tenors happened to be singing that night. My thoughts of everyone walking around in Mao Zedong green uniforms was certainly off base, even the people riding bikes were dressed to the hilt. Mr. Gary said there are only about 60 million card-carrying communists, but they run the government. The business-oriented Chinese are more like capitalists and just want to make money.

We talked of how I had recently lost my only son and how God was closer to me now than ever before even in this wrenching experience.

Gary talked for quite some time on the history of China, the 50 Dynasties, the Ming Dynasty, the rulers, Mao and the people's plight. As we approached my hotel I finally had my chance and opened up, "I have something that maybe you could use here in China for yourself or to give to someone who needs it. I reached into my briefcase and said, I have two English/Chinese translations of the Bible I'd like to give to you."

He immediately answered, "Yes! Yes! There are two assistant professors at the college I am visiting in a day. They only have bad Chinese translations, but both had been saying they really wanted good English/ Chinese-translation Bibles! They are very hard to get here in China. They will share these with many people. Thank you very much."

Inside my spirit I was saying, "Praise God! You are awesome!"

As we parted company, Mr. Gary said he would stay in contact with me by email and I thought, "Wow, what a great guy and an important contact in the Chinese world! We'll have to see what develops in the future with this special event."

It wasn't very long before something amazing did happen:

ᛘᚱᚴ

Mr. Li and a Visit to the USA
By Chuck Brockmeyer

The Chinese client, Mr. Li, who owned the edible oil company in Liaoyang, was coming to our company in the U.S. to see our facility, talk about the soybean industry, and view our equipment.

I had read a Bible passage in Romans, that explains why our Christian faith is different from any other type of faith and thought to myself, "This is a statement that would mean something to Mr. Li." So I copied it onto a letter and wrote on an envelope "To Mr. Li, I thought you might be interested in this Bible passage. Your friend, Chuck."

The reason I thought he may be interested in the Bible verse was because of my making a new friend and contact in China, Mr. Gary Hu, who told me that he had been telling Mr. Li that he needed Jesus, explaining the gospel to him in bits and pieces. Mr. Gary would also be coming as Mr. Li's interpreter. I didn't have a clue if I would really have a chance to give the letter I had written to Mr. Li, but I ran a copy anyway and placed it in my work folder in my office.

The Chinese had driven to Minneapolis from Chicago the night before and now we were shaking hands in one of our conference rooms and introducing ourselves. Chris, the vice-president of the Oil Seed Department, left to get some presentation material. There we were, sitting together at the large conference table, the Chinese and me when Mr. Gary said, "This is the good person I told you about, my Christian brother, Chuck." Everyone smiled widely. By their expressions I thought they were all Christians, too, so I say to Mrs. Luo, a commodities agent and friend to Mr. Li, "Ah, you are a Christian, too?"

"No", she said, "I am a Buddhist."

"But she is very close!" Mr. Gary broke in. Gary and I laughed and patted each other on the back.

Everyone smiled and I thought, "What is going on here? This is kind of strangely wonderful the way this whole thing is going. God, this is really great!"

I had to get some papers from my office and left the conference room. I remembered the letter I had written and thought, "If God wants me to give this letter to Mr. Li, I will give it to him." I put it into my folder and headed back to the conference room.

As I walked, I prayed about it again only because I was worried about who Mr. Li really was. Chris built up such a bad reputation around Mr. Li, I thought I was dealing with someone from the Chinese Mafia. I had my doubts about business in China and kind of bad-mouthed them stating to my project manager, "Isn't China still America's enemy?"

He said to me, "No, they are not our enemies. They only want to make money and they don't look at us like the old communists did."

"Oh, OK," I relented. I prayed again, "God, please prepare Mr. Li, Mr. Gary and Ms. Lou's hearts for our company and our hearts for them." I let my fear go, and felt whatever God has planned I am OK with it.

The meeting seemed a success. We toured our company's fabrication shop and saw the machinery Mr. Li was interested in. We ate at a beautiful golf club restaurant looking out on the rolling manicured lawns. I had a great walleye lunch and listened to all the interesting stories about the largest soybean crushers in the world. I thought back to having gotten a job at such a great company as Buhler Inc. and how God had worked out the details in having me fit into my position, which is a different story. Our company was one of the biggest suppliers of equipment and processes for the world's oil seed producers. Being a Swiss-owned company in the USA and located centrally in Minneapolis gave us a good location as the competency center of oil to the world. We all had very good conversations.

Back at the office I needed to say my good-byes, but I remembered my letter for Mr. Li. I went to my office to grab the letter. I was a bit afraid, my heart was pounding, but I said, "OK, I'm going to just walk right in there and talk to Gary. If everything is right it will just work out."

Folding the letter, I walked up and said to Gary, "If you think it is OK and won't offend Mr. Li, I'd like to give…" Gary grabbed my letter before I could say anything else, opened it and started reading. Without hesitating, he handed the letter to Mr. Li who read it and with all gravity said, "Thank you very much." I was truly surprised because I had never heard Mr. Li utter any English words before. Mrs. Luo said, "Oh—where's mine?"

It was time for them to head to the airport and we said our warm good-byes.

Nothing warms my spirit more than the inner excitement that God used me for something special.

ℰℭ

A Path Lit by 133 Stars
By Ed Mickolus

On my first day as an employee of the U.S. Central Intelligence Agency, I followed many others over the years who walked into the main lobby of the Original Headquarters Building in Langley, Virginia. No matter what your reason for entering on any given day, your eye is drawn to the Memorial Wall on the right, highlighted by several rows of 133 stars. Beneath it is the Book of Honor, which names many, but not all, of the individuals who are memorialized for their ultimate sacrifice to our country. Even in death, their identities must be protected.

The 133 died in service in numerous ways—embassy bombings, aerial hijackings of their flights, air crashes, gunfire while waiting to turn left from Route 123 into the Headquarters compound, in other terrorist attacks.

Virtually everyone in the Agency knows someone now forever remembered on the Wall. The Agency is a comparatively small organization, and its officers develop a tight-knit network. The Stars I knew directly included two whose CIA 101 entry-on-duty class I addressed, an officer who worked for me on one of his first interim assignments, and a woman who played third base on an Agency softball team I coached.

What brought them here? What led them to sacrifice their lives for a greater cause?

Perhaps their motivations in joining the Agency were similar to mine, or to the hundreds of applicants I interviewed during the years that I served as a recruiter of the next generation of American heroes.

As I took advantage of numerous opportunities the Agency offers in developing skills, trying new things, and have experiences I never expected, I always kept in mind the sacrifices of those heroes.

I first became aware of the possibility of becoming an Agency professional when I was pursuing my doctorate at Yale. PhD school generally prepares you to address 18-year-old faces for your career as a university professor. But a fellow grad student told our classmates about his summer graduate fellowship at the Agency in its analytical directorate. He used the skills and tools he had developed in the classroom and applied them to real-world analytical problems rather than lecture notes. He was enthusiastic about his experience, and had already arranged to return for a second fellowship.

Having grown up seeing only James Bond, Napoleon Solo, and others on TV and the movies as the role models for intelligence officers, I was intrigued that one can serve one's country by intellectual inquiry, rather than operational derring-do. So I applied and to my surprise, was accepted.

It soon turned out that my friend was correct. I used exactly the skills and knowledge I'd developed in writing my MPhil thesis and PhD dissertation in preparing analytical papers that went to the seniormost policymakers in the U.S., including the President, Cabinet members, Senators and Representatives, generals, and various other worthies. I was surrounded by patriots who devoted their careers to ensuring that the best intelligence was collected, analyzed, and provided to those who were called upon to make informed decisions on behalf of the American people.

Secondary benefits of an analytical career for me included the opportunity to know virtually everything that is known about a particular topic. One can overlay what is available in the academic and research worlds with the various sources of classified intelligence — human source, intercepted communications, diplomatic and military collection, measurement and signature intelligence, and nowadays, digital methods — to divine the most comprehensive picture possible of what is going on, and what it means for U.S. policy choices. For someone fascinated by detail but also the Big Picture, it was the perfect environment for me.

The Agency gave me an opportunity to use my quantitative skills in analyzing international terrorism, my regional knowledge in looking at African political issues, and my background in psychology in looking at world leaders' decisionmaking styles. As an analyst, I had the opportunity to meet with foreign heads of state and cabinet officials, travel the world, and be a small part of history. It was all heady stuff for a kid from suburban Michigan…

Having established that I could make a difference as an analyst, I wondered if I could also be of use in operations — collection, counterintelligence, and covert action. So for another decade of my career, I conducted collection and covert action operations at the direction of the President against terrorists, narcotraffickers, regimes developing weapons of mass destruction (including nuclear, radiological, biological, and chemical weapons and methods of delivery, such as missiles), rogue nations, and other no-goodniks. The effects of these activities saved American lives in numerous cases and contributed to making the world a far safer place. During this period, I served with the Special Activities Division, which has, alas, contributed the most stars on the Wall.

The Agency later tapped me to work on internal communications, as I could speak two of the Agency's specialized languages — analysis and operations. I had the opportunity to tell the stories of heroes from across the Agency and learn how Agency leaders solved problems and dealt with the highest levels of government. It gave me a fly-on-the-wall view of virtually everything the Agency, and by extension, the foreign policy and defense communities, became involved in during my tenure.

In my 33 years at the Agency, I dealt with three American presidents, countless service chiefs and cabinet ministers overseas and in the United States, billionaire captains of industry, ambassadors, generals, Hollywood celebrities (who viewed us as the real stars — they were just portraying us), sports Halls-of-Famer members supporting our charity events, and the most clever, driven, dedicated civil servants anywhere in government.

I believe that the 133 stars found at the Agency what I did — a cause greater than ourselves, a camaraderie unmatched anywhere in government or the private sector, and a chance to see, and sometimes formulate, history. Agency officers get the opportunity to serve the American people in unique ways. The public will probably never know what the 133 stars, and Agency officers in general, did and do, respectively, but they can sleep better knowing that we're looking out for them. A heartfelt thanks to the 133 who inspired me during my career.

Notes for your memories of this age:

I MATTER TOO!

CHAPTER 5

The Age of Sharing: Family / Marriage / Children

℥℣

Expeditious Adoption
By Rick and Nancy Banks

Rick: It was January 1983 and I was showering in my stateroom aboard a U.S. Navy frigate operating off the west coast of Central America. My phone rang (actual phone, cell phones didn't exist yet). As executive officer I was in touch with most things happening on the ship. I was pretty sure there was nothing going on to require me to get out of the shower.

As I was dressing there was a knock at my door. I opened it to find the captain standing there. He said, "Rick, we've got to get you home!" My reaction was, "Oh no, who died?" That would normally be the only reason one would be leaving during a deployment.

He said, "No one died. You're going to be a father!" Rather stunned, I replied, "Wait a minute, we left homeport three weeks ago and I'm pretty sure Nancy was not pregnant." He said, "No. You're going to adopt, but it can't happen unless you're there."

Nancy: I had been talking to adoption agencies and lawyers about adoption. We both very much wanted to be parents. We had had three pregnancies that went nearly full term, but for three different reasons the babies did not survive. They never made it out of the hospital.

I learned that there was a lawyer in town who had a baby for adoption. He indicated that there was already a couple interested in the child. I met with him and after about two hours he said, "Well, the baby is yours, but you've got to get your husband home."

I told my story to the captain's wife who was a good friend, and a mother of four. She contacted the Navy chain of command who sent a message to the ship.

Rick: Two days later the ship pulled into Panama to refuel. I went ashore and was lucky enough to hop a military flight to Charleston, via Puerto Rico. Two other guys from the ship and I landed in Charleston, about midnight. There was no other way to get out of town except to rent a car, which we did. They dropped me off in Atlantic Beach at about 5:00 a.m. on a Sunday.

I was amazed at how this happened so fast and that it happened at all. We had to quickly set up a nursery and stock supplies needed for a new baby. We had purchased some items during the previous unsuccessful pregnancies, but it was a whirlwind. It was a rush because the state Family Services inspector was meeting with us at the house on Tuesday afternoon.

We met with the state representative who questioned us for about two hours. After that she said, "You can go pick up your baby." We jumped into the car and did just that.

The hospital could not release Jeff to us, only to the lawyer. We waited in the lobby while the lawyer went up to get him. Next thing we saw was the elevator doors open and there was the lawyer holding Jeff and sitting in a wheelchair. Some rigid policies never change.

We got Jeff home, fed and changed. A longtime friend, mother of four, stopped in to see our new addition. We asked, "Well, what's next?" She said, "Go to bed. He's going to be up in four or five hours looking for food." That's the way life went for the next few months.

In early May we went before a judge who pronounced Jeff legally ours. It was just in time because the very next day the packers showed up to ship our household things to Guantanamo Bay, Cuba, our next duty assignment. Jeff lived there with us for the next two years.

From the minute we first saw Jeff to this day we know God has blessed us with the most wonderful addition to our lives.

Nancy: God has truly blessed us with the gift of our son, Jeff! But it all started on a Thursday morning when I was at tennis practice. It was the same Thursday Rick was in the shower. One of my friends came over to me and excitedly said, "Nancy, call this lawyer, he has a baby available for adoption!" And so, I immediately called him and thankfully he agreed to meet me at noon. We talked for about two hours discussing my wonderful 14 years of marriage to Rick and where the Navy had sent us, our loving and supportive families, and finally all my failed maternity experiences. Well, I can't tell you how shocked I was when the lawyer stood up, ending our conversation and said, "The baby is yours! If you want to see him, he is at St. Vincent's Hospital in the maternity ward." Of course, I rushed right over there and asked to see Michael Allen. When the nurse held him up at the window, I just cried for joy! There is my baby, just two days old I sobbed! It was love at first sight and five days later he was in our home in our loving arms and hearts forever!

Only our Lord and Savior could have arranged for the pieces or details of our lives to change so unexpectedly. From the loss and sadness of not being able to have our own child to the extraordinary experience of being at the right place and the right time for us to be able to adopt. We were given a purpose and responsibility that we have dearly taken on and continue to love!

ॐ)C8

Coast to Coast
By Harlan Rector

On June 29, 1956, President Dwight D. Eisenhower signed a significant piece of legislation which funded the construction of the U.S. Interstate Highway System. By the early 1990s almost 45,000 miles were completed. One could effectively travel on just four interstate highways going from California to New York. That's what the Rector family, plus one, were doing in 1982.

Our family consisted of myself, wife Joan, sons Jeff, Jerry and Doug, daughters Dana and Amy and Ed Park, our son's Korean friend from high school. Ed was a good friend to all the Rectors. He went to a Jewish elementary school at one point, so he often said he was Jewish to broaden his appeal to women. Ed also considered himself as a kind of cowboy. Our creative sons wrote a song and created a video for Ed, complete with a bevy of beauties, titled "The First Jewish Cowboy from Korea," which Ed showed to everyone.

They were all helping us move to Connecticut. The four boys, all in their 20s, would be returning to California and our two daughters would be entering middle school in Connecticut.

Except for the girls, we all took turns driving our caravan which included a four-door Datsun, a VW camper and a fully loaded U-Haul truck. We picked up I-40 in Barstow, California and headed east. Except for our slight detour to visit the South Rim of the Grand Canyon, it was a pretty uneventful trip. After two days we stopped in Oklahoma City for the night before changing to I-44 and on to St. Louis.

We were excited the next morning and talked at breakfast about being in St. Louis by evening. Joan and I grew up in St. Louis, went steady in high school and had lots of friends to see as well as my brother and his family. We decided that I would drive the VW camper along with Amy and Ed, Doug would drive the Datsun with Joan and Dana and the twins, and Jeff and Jerry would drive the U-Haul with Jeff at the helm,.

Doug had studied the AAA map so he would lead the caravan, followed by the U-Haul and me in the VW camper. The interchange exit came up fairly fast so the Datsun was fine but it was a little too sharp for the U-Haul. Halfway through the left turn the U-Haul started wobbling. I was behind the U-Haul and I watched in horror as the truck was now only on the right wheels and the whole right side crashed against a low concrete railing and continued on its side riding on the railing with sparks flying everywhere. Jerry, on the passenger side, looking out his window, was looking straight down to another highway 50 feet below. Luckily, Jeff had his seatbelt on so at least he had his hands on the steering wheel. Watching helplessly from behind, all I could imagine was the U-Haul flipping over the low concrete railing.

Then, the U-Haul miraculously righted itself onto all four wheels and we all managed to slow down and pull over to the left and park on a grassy median strip between the east- and west-bound lanes of I-44. We all got out and gathered around and Jeff, worn out trying to hold on, was almost in shock. I remember saying, "God must be telling us something", and then, Douglas, our 21-year-old son said, "God's trying to tell you He's alive." God's truth, spoken from the humblest one among us. Then Dana, who was in Doug's car said, "I was screaming because Doug was seeing the whole thing through his rear view mirror and was babbling crazy words out loud." That's when we found out that Doug, involuntarily, was speaking in tongues, calling on the Holy Spirit, to save his brothers.

I know little about the spiritual gift of speaking in tongues, but, researching later, I found it has everything to do with the Holy Spirit. I didn't know, none of us knew, until much later, that Doug had at least one other instance when he involuntarily spoke a rebuke of a verbal disagreement that didn't even involve him but, nevertheless, silenced the argument of two friends. Miracles happen every day and can't always be explained. That's where our faith comes in. I believe we all have 'spiritual gifts' of one kind or another and that they are divinely apportioned. We thank God for His gift to Doug.

ℛ℘

Accepting Life's Way
By Tim Watts

An old adage in the financial markets is "don't fight the tape"; go with the direction of prices.

In a much larger context, the same may be said of life. As I have aged my experiences have taught me not to fight life, rather to listen and act.

Countless experiences have provided meaning in my life, though I am a much better listener in my older age than my younger days. Like many, I have been blessed with a good family, special teachers, and caring friends — from whom I learned about the important things in life.

I too have had my share of challenging times such as career setbacks, an early divorce, and loss of loved ones, the hardest of which was the death of a wonderful daughter when she was 28 years old.

Fortunately, by the time Andrea passed, I had learned enough to realize that the way out of deep grief was to find meaning in the loss. My wife and I took it as a sign to recognize our daughter's keen interests in befriending and helping others, especially children. Andrea worked at a latch-key program while in high school and as a summer camp counselor for several years. She married shortly before her death and was eagerly looking forward to having children.

Her passing led us to creating a charitable fund with children as recipients that will continue long after we pass on under the supervision of her three sisters, and eventually as an endowed fund. The Andrea Watts Sparling Fund for Children contributes to a wide variety of children's needs in the U.S. and other countries, including abused and neglected children, girls in STEM (science, technology, engineering, and math), and children with health issues. Some contributions have led to personal experiences for my wife and me, such as visiting the students at dance and art programs with Living Arts in southwest Detroit and hearing the performance of the Jacksonville Children's Chorus.

Little did any of us know that Andrea's ultimate love of children would show forth not from giving birth but rather through support of many we now refer to as Andrea's children.

Aging teaches great concepts and we can find meaning and peace of mind through them.

I am a collector of quotations and one close to my heart is:

"How could I possibly explain the great freedom that comes from realizing to the depth of your being that life knows what it's doing? Only direct experience can take you there. At some point there's no more struggle, just the deep peace that comes from surrendering to a perfection that is beyond your comprehension. Eventually, even the mind stops resisting, and the heart loses the tendency to close. The joy, excitement, and freedom are simply too beautiful to give up. Once you are ready to let go of yourself, life becomes your friend, your teacher, your secret lover. When life's way becomes your way, all the noise stops, and there is a great peace." —Michael Singer

I try to be in the present moment and listen to what the Universe is telling me so that there is a path to follow. A religious person might quote, "Be still and know that I am God." Learn to embrace what happens, not seeking to force meaning into my life, but to allow it in. Listen, observe, act.

Life offers so many opportunities to appreciate. Valuable experiences like working through relationship building, watching children choose their own course, becoming open minded, examining dogma, learning new things, improving health, the kindness some people live with, taking time to enjoy the wonders of nature, reading books, enjoying special experiences with friends, and most importantly learning the value of loving yourself and others. Living for what you can contribute and thereby derive meaning.

That has been my experience in mentoring young women in business — helping others create economic opportunity. It is meaningful to me not only because my spouse and I raised four daughters, and I grew up with five sisters, but because I am able to use my business knowledge in contributing to a greater social cause. Business can be a powerful conduit to improving social conditions, but women have been greatly disadvantaged in the business world. Of course, there has long been the "glass ceiling," but even more concerning in the current economic environment is the discrimination in capital funding. Venture capital flows at a rate above 95% to male-owned business startups. The more women can drive business development and network, the greater the benefits for society, males and females.

I have taught classes through the years at universities and community colleges, and employed young people in my business firm who needed training. But it was through Andrea that I began mentoring others in the business world. While in Andrea's mid-twenties, the event planning company she was working for collapsed financially, leaving many people without jobs. I encouraged her to start her own company, which she did with six other women. I provided some general guidance and they went on to be successful through their hard work and enterprising.

My more extended involvement currently is with my youngest daughter becoming an entrepreneur (adelska.com). She too has focused on building her team with women. This has allowed me to become quite engaged with young women regarding various business components from structure to marketing to responding to economic trends.

I believe that women bring a more compassionate and nurturing approach to business, and often a greater focus on goals other than profits such as community involvement, the environment, and supporting local businesses.

Aging offers me opportunities to contribute to others — when I listen with an open mind — and in this my life has found meaning.

I am extremely grateful.

ഇⓒരു

A Christmas Present from Steven Curtis Chapman

By Harlan Rector

The last thing one would ever want to do, in the middle of a world-wide pandemic, is drive two hours or more to a one-man concert because your daughter wants to see and hear Steven Curtis Chapman. Who?

Since our daughter moved in with us, with her 150 CDs, my wife and I have enjoyed a houseful of music from the big band 40's, to the rock 'n' roll 50's and so on to the present day. Her collection includes many Christian recording artists, among them Steven Curtis Chapman.

Our premium tickets allowed us to attend a pre-concert Q and A with the five-time Grammy winner, guitarist, singer, and songwriter, Steven Curtis Chapman.

The concert, held a week before Christmas, was in Northland Church, a huge, modern auditorium-style church with wonderful acoustics and a sound system that brought his performance right up to the row in front of us. That said, the row in front of us and the row behind us were totally empty and we were the only three seats taken in our row. There was a huge crowd in that auditorium, but the social distancing made the whole event seem more personal.

This whole essay could have easily turned into two pages if I only talked about Chapman's incredible performance, however, a statement he made at our pre-concert chat has prompted me to pass it on to you. Talking about his personal life, he said, "My wife, Mary Beth and I have six children, but my life was totally changed when we adopted three of them." Immediately, I was intrigued and interested in having his story of adoption in this book, knowing that life-changing events is what these "I MATTER" books are all about.

A friend, who is the Director of Development in a women's services company, told me that she has a friend who knows the Chapman family. Weeks went by without a word. I know that God's timing is impeccable but it's just another thing that, at my age, I seem to forget. My co-author and I are closing in on finishing this book when the phone rings and it's my friend. She has spoken to her friend about this book and offers an introduction to her. I called her, knowing that celebrities like S.C.C. are extremely busy and are constantly being asked to write, comment, and publish articles about themselves, their life and careers. This very nice lady agrees to forward to the Chapman family all my attachments to her that explains everything about this book and why S.C.C.'s story should be a part of it.

I've been blessed with a somewhat creative mind which leaves no room for more useful, practical things like being able to balance a checkbook or how to read and follow instructions. I believe ideas are a gift, sometimes delivered with a velvet touch and more often than not, lately, with a sledge-hammer. As soon as I hung up the phone, I thought, felt, heard, "Stop trying to force people to fill your book with a story you already know. Get out of your recliner and write it yourself. Be a messenger, not just a delivery boy. BANG." I sent an email to my friend's friend and told her that all she had to do was get Steven and/or Mary Beth Chapman to read and agree to publish this Christmas Present Letter from his wife.

A Letter from Mary Beth Chapman

Our adoption journey began many years ago. God used our daughter, Emily, then a teenager, to speak His will into our lives. He opened our eyes to the needs of children who had been orphaned. Once we saw, there was no choice but to act.

Maybe the reason you're reading these words is that God is doing a similar work in your life. He's calling you to action. He's inviting you on a life-changing journey that will be crazy, beautiful, painful, hopeful, and so many other things. Adoption is beautiful, but it is also hard. And it's a path best traveled together.

My husband, Steven Curtis Chapman, and I founded Show Hope in 2003 because we believe every single child needs to know the love and permanency of a family. Our part in that, outside of our own adoption journey, is to help break down barriers between waiting children and loving families. One of the ways we do that is through Show Hope's Adoption Aid grants, which have helped more than 6,800 children come home to families.

If you feel God guiding your heart to adopt, be encouraged. Even when it seems impossible, there is hope. And there is help along the way!

Adoption Aid grants are the cornerstone of our work and the original vision of our founders.

One of the primary barriers standing between waiting children and families is the cost associated with adoption. Our grants help break down that cost and have been a part of helping more than 6,800 children come home to the love, security, and permanency of a family.

૭૭

A Tragic Accident
With a Happy Ending
By Diane Quick-Machaby

I've heard many times through the years, "It's always in God's time, not mine." This story shows firsthand how God is at work in our lives. It was only through His miraculous will that this series of incidences could occur.

On New Year's Eve 2004, as I was traveling north on Interstate 95 from St. Augustine, I saw a huge plume of smoke in the sky ahead on the interstate. I immediately said to myself, "Oh, Lord, I hope that's not an accident" and said a quick prayer for anyone who might be involved in the accident.

Shortly thereafter, with smoke still billowing, the traffic came to a halt and Life Flight helicopters landed to airlift the injured. I knew it had to be a bad accident but when I arrived on the scene, I never saw a more horrific sight.

The van that a family had been traveling in had caught fire upon impact and Fire Rescue personnel were now scraping the interstate from where everything within the vehicle had melted. I knew there were serious injuries, maybe even casualties. I said another prayer for this family, whoever they might be.

The following day, I read in the newspaper that the family in the accident, a mother, father and six children, were traveling in two vehicles. They were moving back to Ohio because they could not find jobs or housing in St. Augustine they could afford.

As I suspected, one of the children, the oldest son, had died in the fire. One daughter was critically injured and two others were seriously injured. A benevolent fund was started to help the family with medical expenses, so I sent in a contribution. I also decided to write to the Extreme Home Makeover television show about trying to help this family by building them a home. Unfortunately, I never heard back from the show. Time passed and I didn't hear anything more about the family either, but hoped that somehow, someway, someone would help them. Little did I know that someone was going to be me!

A year and a half passed and I was sitting in my office at Habitat for Humanity in St. Augustine when I overheard a conversation by a woman who had come in and was telling our receptionist the same story. She was the oldest daughter of the family who had been in the horrific accident. Heather Gaughan, age 26, told of the accident, of how her parents had abandoned the children and how she had recently gained custody of all of her five siblings.

The story broke my heart, but I did not step out of my office to say I had seen the accident, that I had sent in a check or that I had contacted the television series. Heather Gaughan sounded like one of the most responsible 26 year olds and I wanted her to apply for a Habitat for Humanity home without any of my influence or encouragement. I did not want to get her hopes up in case, for some reason, she was not qualified. She began the application process that day and within a few short months was accepted into the program. Clearly, I could see this was no coincidence and that God had His hand in this.

Heather and her siblings would need a six bedroom, handicap-accessible home because not only did she have three siblings who were developmentally-challenged but she also had a 13-year-old sister who had to have one lung removed and a foot amputated after the accident. This sister would one day be in a wheelchair and we wanted to plan for that.

The home Heather was renting at the time was far too small for her new family. In addition, the owner had recently placed the home on the market. Concerned that it might sell quickly and Heather and her siblings would become homeless, I immediately began putting together plans for a blitz build. In Habitat for Humanity terms, this is the building of a home on an accelerated construction schedule.

Our Habitat for Humanity affiliate didn't own a parcel of land large enough for the six bedroom handicap-accessible home that the Gaughan family would need so I approached the director of the St. Johns County Housing Department, Tom Crawford, about donating a lot to the family. Tom was a close business friend of Habitat's, very kind-hearted and always wanting to help others. He got back to me within two days and stated that the County would donate a parcel of land for the family.

I knew we would need a substantial amount of money to build such a large home so I met with Derek May, the publisher of the St. Augustine Record. The Record had run articles about the Gaughan family and the accident so they were aware of the circumstances and felt a personal connection to them. After checking with the president of their parent company, Morris Communications, the St. Augustine Record agreed to sponsor the home at the full amount of $75,000.

That afternoon, I called one of Habitat's Board Members, Dennis Ginder, who was division president of Mercedes Homes. Dennis agreed to supervise the build, stating that his company had participated with Extreme Home Makeover in Orlando the previous year and he knew they would be on board with the project. Dennis committed to providing the volunteers needed and he actually thanked me for asking Mercedes Homes to be a part of this special build!

A few days later, I received a call back from Shands Jacksonville, the hospital where the Gaughan children had been cared for after the accident. They, too, committed to send hundreds of volunteers to help build the home and would provide lunch for everyone on site each day.

Donations of money and materials poured in over the next few months and in the spring of 2005, a six bedroom, 1600 square foot, handicap-accessible home was built for the Gaughan family during a seven day blitz build in St. Augustine. It was amazing to see the home go from a vacant lot one day to a fully-built, brand new home one week later. At the dedication, hundreds of people came to see the finished product and to wish the family well.

Heather Gaughan is truly an amazing woman who accepted the responsibility of raising her five siblings. Since then, she has become a wonderful Habitat for Humanity homeowner (as I knew she would be), and she and her siblings continue to volunteer with the St. Augustine Habitat affiliate. I am so very thankful that God lead Heather and her family to our door and that He blessed all of us with this miracle!

Editor's Note: An earlier version of this chapter appeared in Diane's *When God Showed Up: Recognizing His Hand in Our Lives*, 2016

∮℣

Lessons from My Mother
By Sue Jones

In the musical *South Pacific*, Emile LeBecque and Nellie Forbush fall in love. Then they hit a snag when Nellie learns of Emile's deceased Asian wife and his children. Nellie muses about her own reluctance to love and accept them and her struggle with her family in Kansas. Emile sings to her, "You've Got to Be Carefully Taught".

I think about the problems in our country centering on race relations and wonder how I arrived at my own attitudes. Then I see clearly my Mother's face, and remember her words.

Born in 1943, I grew up in the aftermath of World War II. Relatives who had been in the Navy visited our apartment with stories of the atrocities of the Japanese. I knew these people were scary and looked different from us. I shivered when my parents took me to a Chinese restaurant; I clutched my Mother's hand as we walked past the beaded curtains. She hugged me and told me that not all people who come from Japan are bad, that the people in the restaurant weren't even from Japan. She told me not to be afraid of people because of how they look on the outside.

We lived on the south side of Chicago, and racial tensions were growing. I heard neighbors talk of the "coloreds" taking over and people having to move. I heard bombs had been planted in the yards of homes a few blocks away. Bombs meant war and I was frightened. One day when I was in third grade I went to school and we had a substitute teacher. I never liked substitutes because they didn't know how to do things like our real teacher. This one was even worse—she was "colored". At lunch time I walked home from school crying; I would not go back to school in the afternoon. When I got home Mother dried my tears and wanted to know what was the matter. I told her about the scary substitute and pleaded not to return to school. She hugged me and said that she was sure the substitute was very nice or the principal would not have let her come. I went back to school and we drew pictures. I drew a picture of the teacher, using my brown crayon to color her skin.

We moved from the apartment to a big house and my mother had a lady come to help clean. Rose rode several buses to our house and back home. The day before she came I had to clean my room so it wouldn't be so hard for her to dust and vacuum. Then Mom and Grandma would plan the menu — what Rose would like for lunch and some sort of special dessert. One day Dad came home for lunch. We were all seated at the table eating and Mom made a place for him. That evening I heard him tell Mom he wasn't sure it was right that his children should be eating with the hired help. Mom rarely contradicted Dad, but this time she was adamant. Rose was her friend, she worked very hard and there was absolutely no reason why we shouldn't all enjoy lunch together.

My childhood was filled with incidents not so politically correct. I treasure all of them. Grandma read me the tales of Uncle Remus and the story of Little Black Sambo. We sat around the radio listening to Amos and Andy, and laughing at the antics of Kingfish. When the much-awaited baby was born on the show I got a little brown Amos Andrew doll. Years later I returned from college to find Amos Andrew missing. Mom had given her to Rose because she had a grandchild and there weren't any "colored" dolls for sale then. When I was old enough I went to the library and took out the *Adventures of Tom Sawyer* and loved his encounters with Huck and Jim, and Injun Joe.

I lived through the change of terminology from colored people, to Negro, to Black, to African American, to people of color, which sounds a whole lot like the "colored people" I first learned.

I've always been glad I am just stuck with American—not French, Irish, English, Native American, American. I wonder if "people of color" wouldn't prefer it that way.

In my grown up life a college roommate told me to be sure to wash the pan I lent to the colored people across the hall when they returned it. In 1965 I was planning to drive across the country from California and a black teacher friend was headed the same direction. I suggested we share the drive. Her answer was, "Honey, do you want to get us killed? We can't drive across the South together." I have had friends who contemplated interracial marriage, and faced pressure from family and friends and one who did marry, and drifted apart from us.

I have seen laws change, tensions in cities where I lived ignite, ebb, fall, flare up. I taught children in special education classes who were often racially and/or culturally diverse. I have never attended a rally, or supported political candidates for their views on racial justice. I hope I have lived my life with kindness and fairness to all people. I respect the accomplishments of our forefathers—imperfect men living in a different time and place. I tried to teach my sons the lessons I learned from my Mother. I hope children everywhere learn how to love from their mother. I think my earliest lesson, "Don't be afraid of people because of how they look on the outside" was the most important.

∽∝

The Letter
By Anni Rawcliffe

I came home from work on a Friday afternoon in April 2009, and yelled "Hello!" to my husband, Jack, who was, as usual, at the computer in our office. As I did every day when I got home, I plopped my briefcase on the chair in the kitchen and thumbed through the mail that was laying on the counter. It was the usual stuff... credit card giveaways, advertising flyers, a utility bill... and a plain white business envelope, addressed to me, handwritten, with no return address. This was odd!

The postmark was from Copenhagen, Denmark, the place of my birth. I was still writing to a friend from nursery school, and also one of my cousins, and at first I thought it might be from one of them. However, it had been a long time since we had actually written letters, rather than emails, and I didn't recognize the handwriting. Who could this be? So I ripped open the envelope to find a plain white piece of paper, with several typed paragraphs.

For some reason my hands were shaking. What was this? The paper was bouncing in my shaking hands, so much that I had to flatten it on the counter to hold it still enough to read.

The letter started out, "Dear Anni..." and went on to say they were two sisters, Bente and Pia, who then went on to introduce themselves as MY SISTERS! Wow! Deep down in my soul, I had always known that this day might come. How-ever, I had not thought about it for many years, and, for this day to finally arrive... honestly, it was a shock.

Bente, Pia, and Anni in 2010

When I was 8 years old, after my mother had divorced my father, she emigrated to the United States, taking me with her. Apparently, it had not been a "nice" divorce, as she would get very upset every time I asked about my father. After a while, I stopped asking. She eventually remarried, and I thought of her new husband as my father. A few times through the years, I did make attempts to find my real father, but my heart wasn't in it. My new father meant the world to me, and the last thing I wanted to do was have him think I didn't appreciate him and all that he had done for me. I always knew that there was a possibility that I had siblings. And, here they were.

My life completely changed after the letter arrived. For several months after receiving it, I felt like I didn't know who I was any more.

It was a strange feeling, even a bit unsettling at times. If someone had said that to me before "the letter", I would have thought they were making too much out of nothing. What does it mean to not know who you are? It sounds rather self-indulgent. I had never dwelled on my family circumstance, other than accepting what it was. I was simply a daughter in a family with a much younger brother, then a wife, a mother, a grandmother, but never one of three sisters. This was how I had defined myself. Now, who was I?

After the letter, I felt different. To think that my world now included two sisters, something that made me feel like a different person; it was disconcerting. I had difficulty even letting those words roll off my tongue, as it felt unnatural for me to say the words, "my sister." I had lived 61 years of my life without uttering those words, and it took me a while to become comfortable with this new reality.

I immediately emailed Bente, and we spent the whole weekend with back and forth emails. Bente came to visit me four months after that letter. Either she, or Pia, or both, have come to visit me every summer since. Various trips have included husbands, children, and grandchildren. Unfortunately, I was never able to meet or talk to my father, as he was very sick at the time of the letter, and he died two months later. However, my life is now much fuller, part of a much bigger family, the kind of family I always wanted.

Notes for your memories of this age:

I MATTER TOO!

CHAPTER 6

The Age of Reflection: Retirement

ॐ

My Life as a U.S. Census Bureau Enumerator

By Susan Schjelderup

Motivating

Public service to the missions of various Federal entities was the shining lodestar for decades of my professional energy. The U.S. Senate, the Congressional Research Service, the U.S. Navy and other Department of Defense organizations, the Department of Energy, Federal Aviation Administration, and the Merit Systems Protection Board received my analytical drive and loyal commitment. As a former Quality Assurance Manager, I value accurate and useful data and the information it creates, as all who know me will confirm. They might even say, *inordinately* value!

Collecting data for a higher purpose was my motivation for becoming a U.S. Census Bureau enumerator. Many Americans don't realize that U.S. Census data drives Federal aid to their own communities. Some 1.5 *trillion* Federal dollars have been allocated to states and local communities based on the 2010 data. Florida alone lost 20 billion dollars from an undercount in that census. This Federal money is disbursed to citizens receiving Medicare Part B, Medicaid, unemployment insurance, National School Lunches, highways, fire stations, relief to victims of crime, and so much more.

Preparing

Having an identity crisis was not what I envisioned when I applied to become a U.S. Census Bureau enumerator in November 2019. Nor did I expect the surprising range of my emotions when I finally got into the field in August 2020 to start my census interviewing. I felt joyful anticipation, delight, appreciation, fun, failure, fear, surprise and shame.

Training to become an enumerator prompted the identity crisis. It wasn't difficult content that drove me to tears, but the illogical progression while trying to beat the clock. My brain simply could not remember the sheer volume of bureaucratic regulations and infinite-seeming programming steps. The 2020 census enumerators faced twenty hours of online training compressed into no more than six days, whereas the same training in 2010 took three weeks! My utter frustration led to the identity-shaking realization that I was just not a smart person after all. Seeing my anguish, my family urged me to quit.

The crux of the Non-Response Follow Up (NRFU) program was to interview residents who had not completed their U.S. Census survey. I soon discovered what being bi-polar must feel like.

The biggest high was actually completing an interview and closing the case. One day you were at a peak, feeling like a bounty hunter after having read a previous enumerator's case notes that said "Address not found" and then feeling jubilant when actually finding that address and a resident willing to answer questions. But the next day your mood descended further with every door that slammed in your face. I'm a petite woman of a certain age, certainly non-threatening, but sadly, I met more distrustful door slammers than civic-minded respondents.

Interviewing

My daily Case List took me to the richest as well as the poorest neighborhoods in Northeast Florida. I visited grandly gated communities, shanty town trailer homes, farms, and apartment complexes. I saw the diversity of America in microcosm. I heard America in some of these scenes:

- Told to ignore No Trespassing signs, I did so in rural Hastings. I unlatched the gate and walked about twenty feet onto the property, only to see two pit bulls come charging towards me. Fortunately, there were all bark and no bite. I nervously fumbled for many minutes trying to safely secure the lock on the gate as the dogs snapped and growled on.

- The 84-year-old, wheel-chair-bound man who told me with a wink that his race was hillbilly.

- The woman who refused to answer any questions about her neighbor's household, saying it was "rude". I offered to provide her with the Information Sheet identifying a citizen's legal obligation to answer census questions and the confidentiality with which the data are handled. She not only hurled over her shoulder that she didn't want anything from me, but also said that I was "almost" parked on her front lawn!

- The rundown neighborhood – pickup trucks with gun racks, abandoned toys, and strewn trash – where at both addresses, twenty-something men, tattooed and naked to the waist, answered the door – and "ma'amed" me profusely with extreme politeness.

- The abject shame I felt when interviewing a bi-racial, young mother in a poor apartment complex and asking her to choose between being white or black. There was no bi-racial response option available.

- The mean old woman in a coquina-slabbed home in the deep woods whom none of the previous enumerators found at home. She yelled at me and then apologized, explaining her physical pain. And then, feeling garrulous, launched into an anti-local government diatribe about the street flooding but not getting it fixed. She wasn't even the owner, but an old family friend who was allowed to stay there.

- The lonely woman in a mansion whose birthday it was. Her smiling eyes behind her mask suggested that my visit might have been a highlight of her day.

Swallowing Frustration

Clearing my Case List was a driving ambition! A recurring frustration was trying to progress through the data capture program despite its barricades. In nearly all situations, it prevented me from going to a previous screen to correct a typo. One was also prevented from correcting a resident's misinterpretation of a question, which caused subsequent answer options that then didn't fit the resident. Our field supervisor said that the Bureau didn't trust enumerators to fix errors out of concern that we might fake the data.

Regularly disappointing was finding no one at home and then searching out the required three or more neighbor/proxies. I spent more than an hour searching in a neighborhood that was so far on the wrong side of the tracks that I thought I heard the Deliverance banjos. I bumped over ditches, "swam" through hanging vines and Spanish moss, and stepped on rotting stairs to front porches filled with stained mattresses, ancient washing machines, and mildewed clutter. Caught between duty and self-preservation, I made my choice and declined to find the required three proxies for addresses there. With mounting anxiety, I parked at the next address several miles away. The sudden gun shots at my car turned out to be nothing more than crab apples falling on its roof. Later, I felt ashamed of my fearfulness just because the neighborhood was "lower class" than my own.

The daily jaunt sometimes involved a 105-degree heat index, lightning and torrential downpours, packing a lunch and eating it in my car. I tried to avoid zany comedy as I untangled four straps around my neck: Census bag, Census iPhone, reading glasses, and sun glasses. Reaching into the Census bag for the Information Sheet or Notice of Visit while untangling straps added to the disruption.

There were several mishaps through phone numbers associated with resident addresses in my Case List. These phone numbers were not validated, some probably accrued during the ten years since the previous census.

- After a heavy rain the prior evening, I alerted the person on the other end of the phone about deep standing water touching her home's foundation. Her home, it turned out, was not the address where I saw the water!

- Another resident with a Ring [camera] Doorbell yelled through the device from some other location that she was not interested as I tried to tell her that she had a package and dry-cleaning hanging on her front porch.

- An ex-husband advising sarcastically that his ex-wife could answer her own survey.

Managing

My amazing Census Field Supervisor managed fifty enumerators with the only means available: text message and an occasional conference call. What a challenge to train enumerators over phone lines trafficked with many people speaking all at once! He never met us, never saw us, didn't know our motivations or work styles, yet he managed to offer the right, reassuring word and guidance when things got tough.

He and his fellow Census Field Supervisors held us all together and deserve the highest praise.

My recommendation to the U.S. Census Bureau is to not require enumerators to return to the same address three to six more times. Instead of burning those labor dollars, investing in public service announcements and blasting social media with the benefits of the data might have won more immediate trust among the American public. Despite these challenges, 99.3% of Americans have (as of this writing) completed their census either by mail, online, by phone, or through enumerator diligence.

Serving as a U.S. Census enumerator was a privileged experience, a snapshot of Americans that I value—but might not repeat again!

ʂɔ෬

Four Score and Three
By Sheila Weinstein

The realization of how long I've been around…eighty three years… or more correctly that there's more behind me than ahead is a real shocker. My own aging began to make a big noise in my head when I was about to turn 70. I was trying to write a chapter on aging for my book, *Moving to the Center of the Bed.* I had written and torn up several tries. So I took a walk around the reservoir in Central Park, a place where ideas seem to lie in wait when they see me round the first bend. I wrote the chapter in my head before I got home. Of course I couldn't remember half of it when I did, but I think what stayed was what needed to be written.

I was not raised in a society that reveres age, but one which suffers it, sometimes in silence, sometimes not. What I learned as I grew up was that our "Elders" are not wise to most of us, only wizened. That, in the main, we no longer take care of our own; we assign them to assisted living facilities and nursing homes. I was furious with my parents for putting my grandmother in a 'home' after my grandfather died. I wanted to have her with me and my young family, though I know now that it would not have worked well. Her needs and those of my family would have been at odds.

I don't know that I'm 83 until I look in the mirror. I am, luckily, healthy and strong. But as much as I try not to let them…my thoughts stray to a time when I may not be so. I can get carried away with the 'what ifs' and 'uh ohs' of tomorrow. After all, things fall apart. And, if they do, then what? Well, I'd like to keel over playing a concert in Carnegie Hall; or writing a hot chapter on what 'sexy' at ninety is like. However, chances are it won't happen just that way. I am surprised to find myself smack up against the opposite of what I thought was 'right' when I was young: I don't want to be taken care of by my children or grandchildren. Young lives can be ruined by the needs of an elderly and sick parent, no matter how much they are loved. My plan is to stay the constant mother, wise grandmother and caring friend, to be lovingly remembered, not as a nuisance over whom someone will breathe a sigh of relief when I slip off the planet.

When I sit down to write a blog, a chapter in my novel, or whatever I'm working on, I am never sure where it will lead. Words have a life of their own and lead me down paths I would never have had the creativity to envision. So to what conclusions has my unbound mind led me as I write this piece? Well, for one… that I haven't learned anything new about myself since that chapter I wrote on Aging. I believe now what I believed then, only more so: That to live my life to the fullest before the big black curtain comes down and the show is over, I want:

- To accept with grace and dignity the life that is mine.

- To befriend the fear of aging and dying, making it serve me by helping me to live in this moment, and the next and the next.

- To do everything within my means to fill myself with all the things I love.

- To be loving and giving to everyone I meet each and every day, including animals who are people too.

- To remain creatively alive. To finish the work I have begun, and to do the next thing I want to do.

- To be with people I love and who love me.

- To be able to say at the end of each day: "Thank you for another day. I've done all I could do."

I can't know whether, to paraphrase Dylan Thomas, I will go 'gentle into that good night' or 'rage, rage, against the dying of the light'. I tend to think it will be the latter, as I think I will always have more I want to do, and besides, I like it here. But, until then, I intend to continue forward, my glass raised, reciting the wonderful French toast: "Pour la vie…come il vient!" To LIFE… as it comes!

Maybe if I 'wish upon a star' I'll get what I want…to be lovingly remembered, not as a nuisance over whom someone will breathe a sigh of relief when I slip off the planet.

❧⨯❧

The Cross, the Rosary
and a Mickey Mouse Watch
By Sue Jones

Each summer devastating fires, hurricanes, and tornadoes permeate the news. We are assaulted with warnings of items to prepare for evacuation. I dutifully collect the necessities, then wander through the rooms of my house, eyeing possessions accumulated in my lifetime. If I feared all would be destroyed, what would I try to save? I settle on three tiny items I could find in a hurry and stuff in my pocket — a cross, a rosary, and a Mickey Mouse watch.

In the jewelry box on top of my dresser is a tiny gold cross Grandma gave me for my First Communion. I remember the special day so well, and my beloved Grandma. I was eight years old and had carefully prepared for the day. I didn't ride my bike or roller skate for two weeks before so that I would not have skinned knees showing under my pretty dress. I memorized my prayers, and we practiced processing to the altar at just the right pace. A wash cloth spread over the water faucets so that no one would take a drink before partaking the Holy Eucharist. I wore my wonderful white dress and veil and felt a special glow inside when I received Jesus for the very first time. Pictures were taken afterward in front of the pink and red peonies. Grandma presented me with the beautiful gold cross. Grandma lived with us and she was my very best friend. She saved her little Social Security check for special presents like my tiny gold cross.

Years melted away and my husband and I embarked on a dream vacation to Rome. We landed on the morning of September 11, 2001. We set off immediately, walking to the North American College to retrieve tickets for the Papal audience the next morning. Wandering the streets all afternoon we stopped to buy rosaries. I was thrilled to find some left over from the Jubilee Year of 2000, with a medal of Pope John Paul II. Exhausted, we ended the day with dinner at a small bar. The waiter brought us wine not ordered, and toasted us, "For you Americans." The bartender tried to buy us another drink, but we were just too tired. Back at the room we turned on the TV and saw collapsing towers. We thought it was a horror movie until we flipped stations and discovered reality. The next morning our audience in St. Peter's square was solemn, with the ailing Pontiff's prayers for peace. I held my rosaries for the blessing. I can quickly find the rosary in my top night stand drawer.

This Spring we returned home from the funeral of my 97-year-old mother-in-law. She was the oldest of eight, born in Kentucky coal country. She raised my husband and his brother in the hills of southern Indiana. She cared for them, worked hard, sewed their clothes from feed sacks, took them to Sunday school, and made notes in her well-thumbed Bible. She also loved to have a good time, and scraped together money to go to Florida. She fell in love with Disney World and Mickey Mouse. She always wore a Mickey Mouse watch. When we visited her at the nursing home and told her we lived in Florida near Mickey Mouse, her face lit up with a smile. Her Mickey Mouse watch sits on our chest of drawers in front of a picture of Mary and a statue of St. Joseph.

My preparations are complete. If we have to evacuate in a hurry, I will grab the Cross, the Rosary and the Mickey Mouse watch and carry them to safety.

Notes for your memories of this age:

I MATTER TOO!

CHAPTER 7

The Age Beyond Memories: After You've Gone

∽∝

They Were Dying To See Me: Vito's Story
By Jack Knee

When people volunteer it is supposed to be giving of yourself, not "what's in it for me?" However, we all seem to get something out of it anyway.

This chapter is part of my book that will deal with the attitude of dying people in a Hospice program. I have no clinical training. I have been an unpaid volunteer with Community Hospice of Northeast Florida for twenty-seven years. Most of my duties have been to sit with a dying person to give the caregiver an opportunity to get out of the house a few hours. The thing that seems to impress listeners of my experiences the most is that none of my more than 125 patients has ever displayed any fear of death on my watch.

I have heard that upon hearing of an irrevocable death analysis many patients go through a denial and rage stage. As it sinks in, many elect to go into a Hospice program understanding that they have to relinquish life-extending treatment. They cannot play it both ways. All seem ready to go and the spirited conversations I illustrate are examples of their attitude. It is not a grim duty I perform or I would have left years ago. Their attitude, conversation and humor rubs off.

All but three of my patients have been male. I have had every race and all forms of Protestant Christian faiths, Roman Catholic, Jews, three Moslems, agnostics and atheists. I have never discussed religion with any of my patients. Our Hospice has access to chaplains if a patient so desires. There is no magic formula of what type of patient seems to be most complacent with a lingering death. They all are. They know they are going down but they are still throwing punches.

Here's one of my most memorable patients, Vito, a retired New Jersey detective winding down from something terrible inside of him. He could still get around but with difficulty. He had a lot of pride and showed me a book and two magazines where the authors claimed he looked just like Sylvester Stallone. When I met him he had a full head of hair and down to his chin he did look like Rocky. But then on down he looked like Barney Fife.

But not his pride nor sense of humor. He said my assignment was once a week he needed me to shop their grocery list for several of the heavier items. Things like those water bottle cartons, a big melon and so on. To add to the dilemma his sweet wife had MS but it was not noticeable. Their son was sixty miles away.

We agreed on a certain day each week I would handle this request. This was in September or October. He then said except for November 21 he would need me most of the day and on into the evening. When he noticed my puzzled look he and his wife burst into a loud guffaw. He then handed me a background sheet of me he had pulled with his skills to check me out and he learned my birthday is November 21. I also had to laugh. A sense of humor is so typical of my patients. I get them when they are past the rage and denial stage.

My wife knows when I put on my Community Hospice shirt and I.D. badge I am on a volunteer assignment. She knows enough not to ask my patient's name but does wonder what the situation is. When I told her about this grocery-shopping expedition she burst out laughing. One reason we have been married for sixty-four years is we know our boundaries. She hates to ask me to grocery shop on the way home. If she has to, one item is o.k., two is getting into hazardous waters and three is critical mass.

Vito gave me his list of about eight items and two fifty-dollar bills. He calculated there need be no left turns, just one store, no coupons... Simple. Nyet. I noticed one item was chocolate energy drink "Ensure" that seems to be a favorite of my patients. So I thought I would start there and build up my confidence. A bag boy pointed out the aisle. However, when I got to that aisle it must have had forty feet of blister pack six packs: brown, red and white. Chocolate, strawberry and vanilla. But then it got complicated. "High energy", "low energy" and sideways energy for all I know. Sweat beads started forming down my spine.

After making that selection I noticed I had passed on the way a section that held trash compactor bags. Vito had marked the size but I was sure they were all the same. After all, they have to fit under a kitchen counter for the gizmo. They had to be the same size, right?... Wrong!

That section looked like a hay bailer hit it with all the inventory tumbled and scattered in numerous sizes. Now my entire back is sweaty.

Eventually I found all eight items and headed back. When I returned to the Hospice, Vito yelped, "where have you been, we thought you would be back in a half hour and worried you were wrapped around a telephone pole." Future weeks went smoother and some items were repetitive. We had some bantering fun. When he got on me I would respond "what is a paisano like you ordering a thirty-inch loaf of white bread with every slice the same size like it came out of Alamogordo?"

About six weeks later the nurse called me about Vito and said "there has been a change in condition with Vito." That's a code phrase in this era of confidence meaning Vito just died. It's usually quite a shock, for my patients seem so full of life the few days before when I last saw them. Not all of course. I have had some comatose patients but was assigned to give the caregiver a break to get outside a few hours.

My Hospice volunteering makes me feel good although we don't go into volunteering for our benefit. I think it is my great respect for the nurses and CNAs that are so dedicated; the terminal patients die in their arms. Obviously a lot of the attention is keeping the dying patient comfortable. I certainly agree but my role is also to give the caregiver a needed break—to get her/him out of the house several hours once a week. They are under an unbelievable strain and in Florida the nearest relative may be in another time zone. The ones caring for dementia, such as Alzheimer's patients, are experiencing life beyond horrible. The patients, the lucid ones, have fascinating career experiences and share how fate intervened here and there. For whatever reason being a volunteer feels comfortable.

ℰℭ

A Parting Gift
By Ed Mickolus

In the first volume of this series of inspirational books, I wrote about how I hope to make a difference in some people's lives even after my death by willing my body to science. Specifically, I will be going to Harvard Medical School (assuming my wife can find enough postage), where budding medical professionals will get real-world training in operating table procedures on real flesh-and-blood, rather than having to rely on mannekin-Americans. Other donors opt for organ donation services, in which they can save on average eight lives and enhance more than 100 via tissue grafts.

Another cadaver donation option is lesser-known, but equally as important. Several universities around the world have developed "body farms", where researchers can study the rate and type of decomposition in various topographical, climate, moisture, and other environmental conditions, including insect and vulture scavenging. Such research allows investigations to determine time and circumstances of death. Body farms can also be used to train cadaver-detecting canines, investigators in clandestine body disposal situations, and search-and-recovery specialists. At the moment, seven such facilities can be found at U.S. universities, offering distinct climactic conditions:

- University of Tennessee Anthropological Research Facility

- Western Carolina University Forensic Osteology Research Station

- Texas State University-San Marcos Forensic Anthropology Research Facility

- Sam Houston State University's Southeast Texas Applied Forensic Science Facility

- Southern Illinois University Complex for Forensic Anthropology Research (they work with pigs as human proxies)

- Colorado Mesa University Forensic Investigation Research Station

- University of South Florida Facility for Outdoor Research and Training

Australia, Canada, and India have similar facilities.

After completion of the decomposition studies, skeletal remains are cleaned and placed in permanent skeletal collections for further research.

Researchers point out that bodies of all ages are welcome. People at different ages will show different levels of disease and injury effects, so a wide selection of donors is welcome.

No matter what you did or did not do in life, no matter how many people whose lives you affected for good or evil, you still have the opportunity to help by donating your body to science. You can still matter.

₨₧

Where Do We Go From Here?
By Harlan Rector

In the King James Version of the Bible, Heaven is mentioned 692 times. An entire book was published by the co-author of this book, Edward Mickolus, chronicling all the recorded words ever spoken by Jesus, which included the 116 times Jesus mentioned Heaven.

Hell, on the other hand, is mentioned a mere 35 times.

There have been countless occasions where individuals witnessed some wonderful glimpse of Heaven, and in many cases, an unexpected encounter with Jesus, and lived to tell about it. That should be good news for any Christian who takes their faith seriously.

There, also, has been frightening, bone-chilling tales of Hell witnessed by some during a near-death experience, that reach deeper into an abyss that any morbid imagination could conjure up. That should scare the hell out of us.

On the opposite side of the question, "Where do we go from here?", is a total disbelief in anything beyond one's last breath.

In 1899, Willard Vandiver, a congressman from Missouri, said in a speech, "I come from a state that raises corn and cotton, cockleburs and Democrats, and frothy eloquence neither convinces nor satisfies me. I'm from Missouri, and you have got to show me." I was born and raised in the show-me state and 'show me' was always a safe way to put off answering tough questions.

Depending on which poll is used, anywhere between 80% and 92% of Americans answer yes to the question, "Do you believe in God?" It's easy to answer yes, but there should be a follow up question. Which part do you believe in? Are you all in with your belief in a God big enough for you, or do you pick and choose a part of God to believe depending on your need at the time?

The problem with picking and choosing parts of God… is timing.

A belief in God is like running down a narrow one-way street. God gave us life to make the journey, Jesus shows us how to navigate the way and the Holy Spirit sets all the green lights in our favor. All that is required from us is that we obey His laws on our way to our destination. However, only God knows when we'll get there. Timing.

Jesus used parables in His teaching and described Heaven and Hell in a remarkable way in Luke 16:19-31 in The Parable of the Rich Man and the Poor Man.

Life belongs to God, the Creator, death as well, but He always leaves the door open for our transition to the Age Beyond.

This book, **I Matter, Too,** features essays honoring some positive action or event that changed a life or its direction, and encourages the reader to chronicle his or her own recollection as well.

Our last breath is not the time to answer, "Show me."

Notes for your memories of this age:

I MATTER TOO!

Epilogue

ॐ

Resilience:
Lessons from a Plastic Clown
By Sheila Weinstein

I took myself to Central Park for a walk on this the first day of beautiful weather after a week of hurricane force winds and torrential rains both of which created havoc in and around the New York City area. Spring was evident in the crocus popping their heads above the soil, daffodils as well, trees budding green. Soon the lush cherry blossoms will be out. And, too, there were felled trees, torn from their roots, branches blown down, but fortunately few in the area in which I was walking. The fact that trees can bud again after such horrendous weather conditions; the fact that sometimes, there is no saving a tree that did not have enough stability to withstand the harrowing natural circumstances, I liken to our human circumstances. Some of us will face disasters, great loss and tragedy... and still bloom. Others may not have the ability to withstand their life circumstances.

It's all about resilience. Surviving loss, moving forward in spite of the daunting circumstances of being left alone, perhaps, as happened to me, late in life. How to learn to be devoted to ourselves in order to find a new life of passion and purpose

Do you remember those plastic blow up toys we used to play with as children? Sometimes they had a picture of a clown on them. We'd hit them hard and knock them to the floor and then slowly they'd come back up to a standing position. Then, POW! we'd give them another blow and down they would go and once more come to a standing position. Not quickly but little by little by little until they were straight up again.

And so it is with life when we are hit hard by circumstances beyond our control. If we care enough about ourselves, we work at bouncing back to a standing position. And that is a big "IF." Initially we feel that we cannot go on. If we have borne the loss of the love of our lives, our partner, the center of our worlds, we feel as if half of us were missing, half our heart, half our soul. We may sit for weeks, months, unable to move out of the terrible feelings of loss and depression. And we feel we don't matter without him or her.

What we must come to understand through the mist of our tears and fears, through the uncertainty and anxiety and depression that accompany our loss is that something precious remains. WE remain. The great love of our lives is gone, the preoccupation of our life is gone and what is left, literally and figuratively is us. We are now the center of our lives and we have to learn to be self-ish in the best sense of the word. Always taught to think of others first, we must now, in order to not only survive but to find a new and rewarding future, dedicate ourselves to ourselves. We have to ask the questions: What matters to ME? What is important to ME? What do I love? What do I want to do? What are my strengths? What makes my heart sing? What makes me feel connected to something beyond my grief and loss?

Within each one of us, there is great treasure to be found. In my own case, my husband's illness and ultimate death were the catalyst for my becoming who I am today. The worst thing to happen to me became the foundation of a new life and there emerged a woman I never knew. I suspect the same will be true for you.

But, beware senseless guilt. There's a great deal of guilt that comes along with being self-ish...centered on our self. Sometimes the guilt is from within and sometimes it comes from those in our lives who think we 'shouldn't' be doing this or that, going here or there, engaging in recreative endeavors, finding new paths. They might wish that we were our old selves, there for them, there to listen, there to heal, there, there, there. Woe to us if we fulfill their wishes!

"Happiness" is illusive. Here today, not so tomorrow. For me life is not about happiness, but meaning. I search every day for what gives my life that meaning, whether it is in a piece of music I compose, a poem I write, feeding someone homeless, reconnecting with an old friend, baking cookies for the children across the hall. I look every day for some way to find in myself the joy of living in whatever form it takes.

But, it's not easy and it takes time to recuperate from the loss. One small step and then another and another. In order to move on we must first feel all the terrible feelings that accompany our loss... the anxiety, depression, fear. And then one day when we open our eyes in the morning we feel better and that's the day to begin to think about what we wish to do in our own interest just for that day for starters...and then do it. See what comes from it. Notice how we feel. And whatever we do feel, make sure it is not guilt. Life put us where we are and as it gave us grief, it also gave us new opportunities. We are meant to take advantage of them. Our time here is short. We all know that. For many of us the years ahead are fewer than those behind us. So, we must make them beautiful and rich.

Find your passions and make them a part of your everyday life. And when you are down, think of the plastic clown, slowly making his way back up to a standing position. That's YOU!

Bravo!

Brava!

Editor's Note: A similar column ran in PsychologyToday.com on March 17, 2010. A poetic version of this article's message appears below:

Lily of the Valley

When I am old, say 83

and freed of all my guilt,

I will not lay upon my bed,

nor sit and sew a quilt.

I'll get me out into the world

of fascinating things.

My age will then excuse my want

for one last big time fling.

I'll go alone, for what's to fear

when now I know for certain,

the next big step is sure to be

behind the big black curtain.

There's much to do and little time

to fill my life with glee.

I must begin by telling you

how I will dress - FOR ME!

No matter where the journey leads,

no matter what the clime,

I'll always wear a big red hat,

and hot pants colored lime.

My ears will sprout outlandish lengths

of plastic fruits and flowers.

My shoes will be of purple suede,

like two large platformed towers.

And on my legs I'll wear no hose

to cover veins of aging.

Instead there'll be a rose tattoo

to keep my hormones raging.

And when I walk, you'll catch my scent

of Lily of the Valley,

that old perfume that once obtained

too many men to tally.

My friends will be the strangest bunch

of people you could think of,

all colors, kinds and attitudes,

some weird, or on the brink of.

And why, you ask, am I so bold

to want to change my self so?

I'll tell you, and please listen well,

you may then wish to follow.

I used to have big strings attached,

and lots of people pulled them.

I danced and sang their tune, not mine,

and smiled a smile that fooled them.

But deep inside that smile turned sour,

and life seemed not worth living,

until I cut those nasty strings,

and gave up all the giving.

The strings are gone, and now I know

how foolish I have been to

deny myself and all I am

for others, kith and kin too.

I tell you friends, it's vital that

you heed those little voices

the ones that say, "Stand up and shout,

I'LL MAKE MY OWN DAMNED CHOICES!"

ℰↄℭℛ

Book Club Questions

I Matter, Too explores how positive events, experiences or people in your life changed our authors for the better or how they helped someone onto a better path.

- Which events come to mind in your life?

- Who are your role models?

- Who has had the greatest influence on your life?

- Did any specific teacher inspire you?

- What is your fondest memory?

- Of those who are no longer in your life, whom do you miss the most? Why?

- Looking back on your life, what is your greatest accomplishment?

- What regrets do you have in life? Is there time/opportunity to fix them? How will you do so?

- What are your goals for the rest of your life?

- What do you want said of you in your eulogy? Your obituary?

- Have you done end-of-life planning?

∾

About the Authors

GREG BARRY

Greg Barry grew up in Fairfax, Virginia. He was an emergency medical technician for six years at Santa Monica Hospital near Los Angeles. Greg earned undergraduate and graduate degrees in health administration while living in California. He met his wife Laura while working at UCLA Medical Center. Greg and Laura spent 20 years living in the Twin Cities working in the health care field. They now live in northeastern Florida.

As a classic film enthusiast, Greg hosts monthly classic film screenings for the nearly 300 members of his community's Classic Films Group. Some of his other interests include literature, post-1950s contemporary music and sports, particularly baseball and tennis. Greg enjoys playing softball, tennis and beach Frisbee.

Greg has joined a talented group of actors from his community as a part-time member of the simulated patient program at Jacksonville University. He works primarily with graduate students in the speech therapy, nursing and psychology departments.

Greg contributed 11 biographies for sketch artist Harlan Rector's *Once Upon a Corner in Detroit*. He contributed four humorous essays to an anthology of essays, poems and reflections in *Riverwood Writes*, published in 2019. He also contributes to a monthly newsletter for a hospice facility in Jacksonville, Florida.

∾

NANCY AND RICK BANKS

Nancy graduated from Pennsylvania State University and the University of Rochester. Because of Rick's Navy career which resulted in eleven different moves, Nancy's teaching experience is quite varied. She taught in many different schools from the very poor to the very rich and in grades from elementary to college. She is a retired college professor. She is also an artist who loves painting beach scenes.

Rick graduated from University of Miami and University of Rochester. He was a career naval officer for 24 years, retired as a Commander, and worked as an environmental manager for the State of Florida.

ℰℭ

CHUCK BROCKMEYER

Chuck Brockmeyer reports that many years ago, I flopped down on a Swiss hotel bed exhausted after 28 hours without sleep. I just flown back from a jobsite in Saudi Arabia where a tough but successful project was completed.

As I laid there in beautiful Zurich, it was though I had landed in a fairyland; clean, organized, full of beautiful people and quaint villages. All this was in stark contrast to the land I had just come from where it looked like the world's largest and hottest gravel pit. I looked up from my bed and gratefully thanked God for all the amazing people, helps and miracles He gave us in making this trip a winner. I asked Him, "Lord, thank you for everything. You are my success, but what can I do for you?"

I heard in my spirit a reply, "Tell people what God has done for you." Then He added, "But know, there will be persecution." That has been the root of my stories and a passion of my life.

Here are a few other steps in my life that I consider less consequential but pretty interesting. Right out of junior college I began working for an architect as a draftsman. I had always been involved in drawing and creative writing so I began studying Studio Art at the U of M in Minnesota. There were more jobs and more years as a draftsman and all of a sudden a big break occurred in my work life. I started a 32-year career with a Swiss-owned company. They placed me at the school of Swiss Feed Technology and I earned the title of Feed Production Engineer and later rose to the title of Industry Specialist. The company sent me all around the world putting projects together and selling their equipment.

My wife and I retired together in 2016 and went happily skipping out the door. My helpful and talented wife of 45 years plus our three grown children have all been a wonderful source of stories, learning, and love through the years. My wife and I now pursue nature hikes and road trips and good food while enjoying Florida's great weather.

Ωℤ

STEVEN CURTIS CHAPMAN

Steven Curtis Chapman was born in Paducah, Kentucky on November 21, 1962 to Herb and Judy Chapman. He attended Heath High School in Paducah, and received the title "Mr. Heath" in his senior year. He wrote and was a songwriter before he made his first CD "First Hand." Since then, he has received 43 Dove awards, five Grammys, and countless other honors. He is known and loved for his style of making his audience feel like they are family. All of these things come together to make him the most successful man in Christian music. Steven has six children, three of which are adoped from China. Their names are Shaohannah, Stevey Joy, and Maria.

MARY BETH CHAPMAN

Mary Beth Chapman is a *New York Times* bestselling author, speaker, and the wife of Grammy and Dove Award-winning recording artist Steven Curtis Chapman. She is the President of Show Hope, an internationally recognized voice for orphan advocacy that she and her husband co-founded, which has given more than 6,000 financial grants, affecting the lives of children from the U.S. and 57 other countries.

ℰℜ

ELAINE CHEKICH

Elaine Chekich reports I grew up the daughter of a Texas farm girl and a steel-worker from Gary, Indiana. Mom was Southern Baptist, and Dad was Serbian Or-thodox. He was first-generation American, and Mom's "people" came over on a ship called the Greyhound in the 1650s. The pair couldn't have been further apart on the cul-tural map. But they met one magical night at a dance, and you know how that goes.

Home life in Southern California was complicated. My three half-siblings treated me with insistent coldness because we had differ-ent fathers. And there was an age difference; my oldest brother was 16 years my senior. Suffice it to say, I was accustomed to being the under-dog, surrounded by big people, big work boots, and big opinions. I had to try hard to keep up.

Story-tellers populated both sides of the family, and luckily, I in-herited the gene. Story became a way of fitting all the pieces together, shuffling them into the big picture. I enjoyed writing, and in time I had the urge to give voice to travelers, past and present, who landed in a wild, fast-lane place like America. When I declared I wanted to be a writer, my loving parents looked at me as if they heard something preposterous, like the Sahara was burning.

I wanted to go to a big, smart college, but rich kids went to them, and there was no money. It was an obstacle, but I'd always felt watched over in my life by a supportive presence that motivated me to strive against the odds. Remarkably, I received a scholarship to the Univer-sity of California, Berkeley. I loved the campus, my literature courses, and I also flipped when I saw Godard's film Breathless. Berkeley was a film-going society, thanks in part to the Pacific Film Archives that showed international films every night. I absorbed massive amounts of global cinema and unconsciously learned the aesthetics of good stories and films. That led me to NYU graduate school in the Department of Cinema Studies, funded by a federal grant.

After receiving my master's, I headed to Hollywood where I worked every film job I could find. When I "temped" for Norman Lear and Alan Horn at Embassy Films, I thought I'd hit the big time for sure. Finally, I got a full-time job at Columbia Pictures under producer Ray Stark's banner. I worked in production on films like *Electric Horseman, It's My Turn* (with Michael Douglas), *Seems Like Old Times, Annie, Wrong is Right,* and others. I gradually moved into putting together feature packages.

Film development is very speculative (read *gamble*). A creative executive can work many months or even years assembling a project that never materializes. The time I spent working in this capacity with talented writers and directors, such as Gore Vidal, Al Pacino, Jonathan Demme, Michael Kozoll, Robert Towne, Richard Brooks, was a golden privilege.

Eventually, I put together a star package with Mariel Hemingway, Warren Beatty, Robert Towne writing, Herbert Ross directing, and the studio greenlighted our comedy romance *Mermaid*.

In a few years, I left the studio system to write. The transition wasn't easy, but again, the voice of faith and support goaded me forward. My fantasy feature script, *Mr. Atlas*, was produced by an independent film company and licensed by HBO and international broadcasters. My first novel *Running Naked* earned representation by top literary agent Alison J. Picard and was optioned (albeit never made) by a producer at Sony Pictures. Many of my feature and TV scripts have been optioned and received awards in screenwriting, including my recent pilot Struck, which was short-listed by the New York Stage and Film Filmmakers' Workshop 2019 at Vassar.

As a writer-for-hire, I adapted the French mystery novel *Zoe La Nuit* as a feature (2015) for Academy Award-nominated director Matia Karrell.

Drawn to teaching, I became an instructor at the University of California, LA Extension in Entertainment Studies (2005-11). I also taught film courses intermittently at Chapman University. At Los Angeles Film School, in the heart of Hollywood, I found a home to teach producing and production as faculty/staff through 2014. I am always thrilled to see the work of my students and graduates now in the industry.

Currently, I am working on a memoir based on my days in the film industry called *Hollywood Fall-Girl* and a comedy screenplay, *Love Hurts*. My short story *Brainzapping on the Metro* will appear in the International Human Rights Art Festival (IHRAF) publication in summer 2021.

When there isn't a pandemic, I split my time between Northeast Florida and Los Angeles.

℘℧

PAT COLLINS

Patrick Collins has been an actor for 46 years. His theatre credits include *Cat On a Hot Tin Roof* on Broadway with Ashley Judd and Ned Beatty, *Mass Appeal, We Bombed in New Haven, A Funny Thing Happened on the Way to the Forum, Dracula, Fiddler on the Roof,* and *Zoo Story.*

Pat's movie credits include *Young Doctors in Love, The Dirt Bike Kid, Mr. Chief Justice, Friends and Family, Exit 10, Jersey Girls, A Fish Story, Sketchbook,* and *Tea at 3:33.*

He appeared on multiple episodes of *Law and Order, Blue Bloods, Shades of Blue, Lights Out, Treme, St. Elsewhere, NYPD Blue, ER, Hill Street Blues, Little House on the Prairie, Dear John, Wonderland, The Chappelle Show, Good Times, The Jeffersons, Give Me a Break,* and the Emmy Award-winning *Juggler of Notre Dame.*

Patrick has been a volunteer Youth Minister for 46 years. For the past 13 years, he has volunteered at Green Haven, New York with RTA (Rehabilitation Through the Arts).

℘℧

SALLY WAHL CONSTAIN

Sally Wahl Constain is a lifelong lover of stories. She was an elementary school teacher and librarian in New York City for more than thirty years. She was president of the Writers Group at Del Webb, Ponte Vedra, Florida for the past three years. She is the author of *The Keys to Fanny*, a work of historical fiction. Her poetry chapbook, *Sometimes I Wonder*, collects twelve inspiring poems on our common human experience. Her latest book, *Random Reflections,* is an anthology of essays and poems, some based on family stories. She is presently writing poetry when inspired by emotions and circumstances, and is working on a sequel to *The Keys to Fanny*.

⅜⅝

JENNY L. COTE

Jenny L. Cote is an award-winning author and speaker who lives in Roswell, Georgia. Her two fantasy fiction series, *The Amazing Tales of Max and Liz®* and *Epic Order of the Seven®*, blend her passion for God, history, and young people. She speaks on creative writing to schools, universities and conferences around the world. Her love for research has taken her to most Revolutionary sites in the U.S., to London (with unprecedented access to Handel House Museum to write in Handel's composing room), Oxford (to stay in the home of C. S. Lewis, 'the Kilns', and interview Lewis's secretary, Walter Hooper at the Inklings' famed The Eagle and Child Pub), Paris, Normandy, Rome, Israel, and Egypt. She partnered with the National Park Service to produce Epic Patriot Camp, a summer writing camp at Revolutionary parks to excite kids about history, research and writing. She earned two marketing degrees from the University of Georgia and Georgia State University. Learn more at www.epicorderoftheseven.com.

JACK KNEE

Jack Knee was raised in Pittsburgh. The year he finished his junior year of high school the Korean War broke out. He enlisted for three years in the Marine Corps and finished as a Buck sergeant. He spent his year overseas chasing the Chinese back up the peninsula. The G.I. Bill paid

Jack Knee with grandson Andrew

his schooling at Robert Morris University in Pittsburgh. He eventually became a CPA and married Carole. Their five children all earned college degrees. In Pittsburgh Jack saw a lot of recessions and a lengthy strike affecting the economy. So he decided to get with something not going out of business, the IRS. This led to moves to Northern Virginia, Fort Lauderdale and Jacksonville for thirty years. Pension in hand, he has had an income tax business for a few decades. He volunteered for such things as church and youth activities, e.g., coaching, band parent, head of church bazaar in Orange Park a few years and the like. He got to like volunteering. With the children raised he felt like trying something different and thought he would spend a few years with Community Hospice of Northeast Florida. That was twenty-seven years ago; it's been a good fit.

₭₨

PATRICIA DALY-LIPE

Patricia Daly-Lipe is an artist and speaker who has written ten books:

- *Miami's Yester' Years: Its Forgotten Founder Locke Tiffen Highleyman*
- *Messages From Nature* (a collection of short stories about animals, the high seas, and nature)
- *A Cruel Calm: Paris Between the Wars* (historical fiction)
- *Myth, Magic and Metaphor: A Journey into the Heart of Creativity*
- *All Alone: Washington to Rome* (a biography)

- *La Jolla, A Celebration of Its Past*
- *Historic Tales of La Jolla*
- *Patriot Priest: The Story of Monsignor William A. Hemmick, The Vatican's First American Canon*
- *Helen Holt: Memoir of a Servant Leader*
- *Horse Tales: Teddy and Just'n Come to an Understanding*

The La Jolla book was the Winner of the San Diego Books Awards in 2002. *A Cruel Calm* (1st edition: *Forbidden Loves*) won the 1st Runner-Up for Fiction JADA Trophy, the USABookNews.com Finalist Award, and in 2013 won First Prize for historical fiction Royal Dragonfly Book Award. She was named Author of the Year 2016-2017 by the International Association of Top Professionals, which gave her a Lifetime of Achievement and Success award in 2017.

She has written for the *Evening Star* newspaper in Washington, D.C., the Beach and Bay Press including *La Jolla Village News* in California, and *The Georgetowner* and *Uptowner* newspapers in Washington, D.C., as well as several magazines across the country.

Her presentations have covered all aspects of writing for literary groups as well as colleges and universities.

In her "spare" time, Patricia has been rescuing thoroughbred horses. In the late 1970s and 1980s, she raised, raced and showed them.

ᘯᘛ

SUE JONES

Sue Jones has been married 55 years to her husband, Bob. She is Mom to two sons, Dave and Jeff. She taught special ed children from pre-K through high school in public and Catholic schools. She was also an educational diagnostician, taught college students studying to be teachers, and supervised student teachers. She also sold real estate, worked for the Chamber of Commerce, and was a teller and opened  new accounts at a bank. The couple moved many times; she cherishes the friends she met along the way, life-long high school and college buddies, and great teacher/co-worker pals. She loves to write stories and poems. Her inspiration is the people she knows and loves.

DIANE QUICK-MACHABY

Diane Quick-Machaby is a native Floridian living her entire life in North and Central Florida. She has two grown daughters and has lived in the Jacksonville area for over 25 years.

After being a stay-at-home mom, room mom, PTA mom, and community activist, Diane got involved in non-profit work in the early 1990s. Over the past 25 years, she's worked in the City of Jacksonville's Keep Jacksonville Beautiful Programs, Habitat for Humanity in Jacksonville and St. Augustine, and most recently with Home Again St. Johns, an agency that works directly with the Homeless of St. Johns County.

In 2015 Diane and her husband started their own business, Art 4 Charities, LLC, which partners with nonprofits worldwide in their fundraising efforts.

Diane and Terry Machaby live with their long-haired calico cat, Scarlett, in Nocatee, Florida, and attend Crosswater Community Church.

⳥⳦

MAL MACIVER

Mal MacIver was born in Brookline, Massachusetts, where free thinking was encouraged. He benefited from having had many mentors during his formative years. He graduated from Northeastern University with a BS in Criminal Justice. He joined the Derry, New Hampshire Police Department in the Fall of 1973. During his 30+ year career, he moved through the ranks to Captain in charge of the operations Division and second in command of the department. Earlier assignments included patrol officer, juvenile officer, detective, patrol sergeant, patrol lieutenant, shift commander, and detective commander. He attended the New Hampshire police standards and training academy to become a certified police officer. He later returned to the academy to teach laws of arrest to new recruits and First Line Supervision to in-service personnel who were in line to be promoted at this academy. He attended numerous in-service training classes throughout the country and is a graduate of the 135 class of the FBI National Academy. He retired in January 2004. He lives in Ponte Vedra, Florida, enjoying the Florida life style, biking, walking, and golfing as frequently as possible. He is an active member of the Riverwood Men's Club and has volunteered for the Players Club Championship for the past seven years.

ℒↃ

JIM MESKIMEN

Jim Meskimen is an actor/impressionist who has been in five feature films directed by Ron Howard, and on TV shows *Friends, The Marvelous Mrs. Maisel, S.W.A.T.,* and *NCIS,* among many others. His impressions were featured on *The View, The Tonight Show* and *America's Got Talent.*

ℒↃ

EDWARD MICKOLUS

Dr. Edward Mickolus graduated from Georgetown University and obtained MA, MPhil, and PhD degrees from Yale University before anyone noticed they were missing. He worked as a staffer at the Central Intelligence Agency for 33 years and as an intelligence contractor for another seven years. He is the President of Vinyard Software, Inc. (vinyardsoftware.com), which produces terrorism events and biographic databases; clients include some 200 universities in 24 countries. He teaches at various universities on writing, creativity, and intelligence. His 40+ books cover such topics as international terrorism, international organization, education, intelligence, history, humor, inspiration, fitness, public speaking, and biography. In addition to the above topics, his 100+ scholarly journal articles and book chapters also cover psychology, law, computers, the Internet, sociology, African politics, folklore, and automobile collection. He is collaborating on several book projects, including his first novels. He has been interviewed by NPR, BBC World, America in the Morning, the *Florida Times-Union*, and the *Ponte Vedra Recorder*, inter alia. For further details, see edmickolus.com and/or his Wikipedia entry.

෨෬

SHERRY-ANN MORRIS

Sherry-Ann Morris is a business and communications strategist with over 20 years of experience in executing communication and marketing strategies, developing brands, business operations and infrastructure, overseeing complex project management, and cultivating relationships with business executives in diverse industries. She is a business owner and consultant who formerly worked as a chief marketing officer, director of external relations and community affairs, and marketing and communications director.

Morris has worked with teens and young adults for many years. She has been on missionary trips that took her to Belgium, Germany, Austria, Finland, Russia, and the Dominican Republic. She has supported, led, and participated in countless domestic ministry groups, conferences, retreats, festivals, and gatherings for children, youth, women, leaders, and business executives. She believes that as great as they can be, they are only truly great when God's presence is powerfully manifested as the main event!

Triumphant Life Verse: *The path of the righteous is like the first gleam of dawn, shining ever brighter till the full light of day.* Proverbs 4:18

෨෬

CAROL SPARGO PIERSKALLA

Carol Spargo Pierskalla, Ph.D., has been a teacher, dean of students and consultant. She was also the National Director of Older Adult Ministries for American Baptist Churches, USA. In the years before her retirement she traveled all over the US, including Alaska and Puerto Rico, teaching, doing workshops and preaching on how to care for the older adults in our communities and churches.

ɬɔʂ

ANNI RAWCLIFFE

Anni Rawcliffe never thought of herself as a writer. She was an accountant that thought about numbers… all the time! Anni had decided, however, when she retired eight years ago, that she would write a memoir. She knew she had a story to tell and wanted her children to know it. Therefore, the first club she joined in her new Del Webb community was the Writers' Group; she felt she needed help! Anni soon realized, however, that she had, in fact, been a writer, unintentionally, all along. She had written a church newsletter for 25 years and a travel blog (jackanni-bucketlist.blogspot.com) as she traveled across the country with her husband, Jack.

ɬɔʂ

JACK RAWCLIFFE

Jack Rawcliffe lives in Florida. He grew up in Rhode Island attended public schools and earned a BS and MBA from the University of Rhode Island. His business career involved managing large and small companies as well as owning an automotive parts business and a manufacturing company. After retiring he started writing short stories about his life as a memoir for his family. This story is from his collection.

ℰℭ

HARLAN RECTOR

Harlan Rector is one of the entertainment industry's best-known voiceover artists. His unmistakable voice has introduced some of the most popular movies, radio and television commercials, and videogames ever made. He was the signature voice of The History Channel during its first four years on the air from 1995 to 1999. Voiceovers were his second career.

He began his first career as an artist in an animation studio, making industrial training films, then made the jump to advertising. As an art director and producer for more than 20 years, he created ad campaigns and won awards for some of the largest agencies in New York, Detroit, and Los Angeles. His voiceover talent was discovered in Los Angeles when he voiced a demo for a Honda presentation. He left art directing, moved to New York, and the rest is voiceover history.

While in New York, he was inspired to create, write, and produce *L.I.G.H.T. (Living In God's Hands Today)*, a dramatic radio series based on true-life spiritual experiences of ordinary people whose lives were changed through the glory of God. The series aired on faith-based radio stations throughout the country, won an Angel Award for excellence in broadcasting and is being developed as a television series. Harlan also donates L.I.G.H.T., in a CD album or via podcast, to prison libraries where inmates can be inspired by listening to stories of how God works in the lives of His people.

He resides in Florida, and at an age when most are enjoying retirement, he's going strong with more projects than ever. He does voiceover work in his specially-designed in-house studio, and he's also rediscovering his artistic roots, creating portraits with oils, pastels, and watercolors. He's an accomplished caricaturist, having captured some of the most famous celebrity faces in the entertainment business.

Harlan has also written and produced *A Taste of Heaven: The Musical*—a joyous and heartfelt musical journey through the life of Jesus Christ. He felt inspired to create this play-within-a-play as an expression of his faith and desire to share with others. He created *Once Upon a Corner in Detroit,* a book featuring 64 celebrity caricatures he drew from life, their bios, and the interesting back story of his inspiration.

For more information, see www.harlanrector.com.

ℂ

JEFF RECTOR

Jeff Rector is an award-winning writer, director, producer, working actor, stand-up comedian and best-selling author. Jeff's first short film *Fatal Kiss*, (a vampire-themed dark comedy), won a variety of film festival awards and is one of the few short films ever acquired by HBO. With the success of *Fatal Kiss*, Jeff created new characters and storyline and expanded it into a feature film, *Revamped,* which touts an all-star cast and was successfully distributed worldwide.

Jeff's other projects include a variety of films, television shows, pilots and a two-season web series. Projects in development include the ski and snowboarding comedy *SnowBunnies*, the Hollywood comedy *Tired of Waiting* and the sci-fi, underwater, action adventure, *Deadly Descent*. Jeff's first documentary film, *Who Is Jeff Rector?* recently won the 2020 Houston WorldFest Platinum Award for Best Short Documentary, Grand Prize Winner at the Golden State Film Festival, Best Short Documentary at The Brazil International Film Festival and Best Editing Award for Action on Film.

As a working actor, Jeff has appeared in over 100 television shows and motion pictures. Notable TV credits include *American Horror Story, The Bold & The Beautiful, How I Met Your Mother, Star Trek: The Next Generation* and *PUNK'd* with recurring roles on *Vice Squad: LA, Reasonable Doubt, Promised Land* and *Black Scorpion.* You can see all his credits at IMDB.com

Upcoming films include the World War II drama *Doolittle's Heroes*, based on true events following the Japanese attack on Pearl Harbor. Jeff plays Rear Admiral Spruance as well as the father of the bride in the romantic comedy *A Walk Down Wedding Lane* for the Hallmark Channel.

Jeff recently released a best-selling book on Amazon, *I Was A Playboy Rabbit and Other Adventures* which chronicles the five-year period Jeff lived and worked in New York City as an actor, eventually being hired by Playboy Enterprises as a Rabbit, the male version of the iconic Playboy Bunny. This was the first time in Playboy's 67-year history that men worked alongside the women. The NYC Playboy Empire Club was also the first Playboy Club to welcome women customers into the nightclub which catered to celebrities, titans of industry and the New York elite. The book also talks about Jeff's experience working with Charlie Sheen and Michael Douglas on the Oliver Stone film *Wall Street* and with Tom Cruise in the Roger Donaldson film *Cocktail* as well as other television shows, films, commercials and voice-overs.

Jeff is a member of the Television Academy and voting EMMY member and serves as the President and Festival Director for the Burbank International Film Festival. Jeff is an award-winning speaker with Toastmasters and is the official spokesman for the Academy of Science Fiction, Fantasy & Horror Films that produces the annual Saturn Awards.

Jeff has served his community on the Board of the Toluca Lake Neighborhood Council and was selected by the Burbank City Council for a four-year term on the Burbank Cultural Arts Commission. Jeff supports a variety of charities and non-profit organizations.

𝄚𝄚

SAM ROBERTS

Sam Roberts, actor, writer, and producer, was born and raised in Montreal, Canada. Sam relocated to New York City more than 30 years ago. In 2011, he returned to Canada to produce his award winning screenplay, *A Fish Story*, a family drama set in wilderness lake country. Sam's love of the outdoors, passion for fishing, and the loving memory of his late father are the inspirations for the film. Sam notes that it is a "film based on a true story about my dad and family with a little 'wouldn't it be wonderful if' thrown in the mix." In addition to writer/producer, the movie also marks Sam's return to working in front of the camera as he plays the role of his father in the film. Sam's background includes many years of working on stage, film and television both in his native Canada and the U.S. In 1984 he turned his energy to the world of voice-overs. His deep, rich, resonant sound made him, almost instantly, the voice of choice for many blue chip accounts. (Some of the countless TV and radio campaigns to feature Sam's voice over the years include: Advil, Aamco, Bank of America, Burger King, Coke, Cheerios, Computer Associates, Capri Sun, Dreyfus, Ford, Hertz, Kodak, Listerine, Lipton, Motorola, Mountain Dew, Magnavox, Nestle, Pepsi, Pizza Hut, Reebok, Reynolds Wrap, Sure Deodorant, Sprite, Sony, Theraflu, Tylenol, Uncle Ben's and Wendy's.) About 20 years ago, Sam turned his focus to announcing on-air promotions for which he has earned a reputation as one of the best in his field. In commercials, he is known for his soft, raspy, cool and sexy voice, yet his strong, 'cut through' style makes his the 'go to voice' when networks want to make a statement through promos. That special ability made Sam the signature voice of TNT Entertainment (Turner Network Television) for 12 years and the promo voice of the NBA ON TNT for more than a decade. Other networks for which Sam continues to do promos include: ABC, CBS, NBC, FOX, ESPN, HBO, USA, TBS, COURT TV (TRU TV), DISCOVERY CHANNEL, MTV, VH-1, HISTORY CHANNEL, and many more.

ℂℂ

SUSAN SCHJELDERUP

Susan Schjelderup reports: I have over 25 years of experience improving operational performance using quality and IT engineering standards, performing quality assurance, survey design and learning technology. I earned an M.P.A. in Policy Analysis and Public Law from George Washington University, as well

as certifications and recertifications from the American Society for Quality as a Quality Manager and Quality Auditor. I applied my knowledge and skills on programs for the U.S. Senate, U.S. Navy, Congressional Research Service, Department of Energy, Federal Aviation Administration, and Merit Systems Protection Board. In retired life, I have taught English as a Second Language to an Iraqi family and managed a community emergency response team. I continue to use quality methods such as preparing process flow diagrams for providing emergency first aid, and a bon voyage party for cherished neighbors; bar charts of most frequent Trivia Nation question categories; and many-factor spreadsheets for buying an SUV.

₧₧

KATHY TRIEBWASSER

Kathy Triebwasser has lived her life inspired by words. This is one of her favorite quotations: *"A hundred years from now it will not matter what my bank account was, the sort of house I lived in, or the kind of car I drove... but the world may be different because I was important in the life of a child."* by *Forest Witcraft, Teacher, Scholar.* She has touched people's lives as a Licensed Marriage and Family Therapist, Life and Wellness Coach, Personal Historian, and Writer. As a poet she wrote and published *Courage Blossoms* and *Do You Know Me, Poems About the Sea.* She is a longtime resident of Ponte Vedra Beach, Florida.

₧₧

TRACY TRIPP

Tracy Tripp was born and raised in Potsdam, New York. She attended the State University of New York at Oswego where she earned her degree in teaching, and then earned her Master's degree in education from Buffalo State College. After one particularly cold winter in Buffalo, she and her husband decided living a bit farther south would be nice, so they moved to Richmond, Virginia where Tracy taught middle school along with various other grades, and they began to raise their family. After eighteen years, she moved to Jacksonville, Florida with her husband and three children. Tracy likes to write stories about the human spirit and the challenges that shape them, but is also open to any whimsical idea that comes her way. Her books include *Parting Gifts, Still Life, Something Like a Dream*, and *The Wealthy Frog*. The sequel to *Something Like a Dream, Awaken,* a children's book titled *Sammy the Snowman,* and a thriller, tentatively titled *White Noise Whispers*, co-authored with Edward Mickolus, are all in the works. Tracy also has a blog that includes interviews with Jacksonville's homeless. Read more about her and her works at tracytripp.com

∾⌓

RUTH VAN ALSTINE

Ruth Van Alstine has been writing poetry since a young age and has seriously pursued a writing career for the past thirty-five years. In addition to her passion for writing, she enjoys handicrafts, jewelry making and trying her hand more recently at collage and acrylic mediums to create artwork in order to pursue a new passion of ekphrastic poetry, which in a simplistic definition is a poem inspired or stimulated by a work of art. She published the popular book of whimsical poems "Fairies and Fantasies" in 1996 and "Shattered Moonbeams" in 2017. She has had poems published in national and international anthologies including "The Parnassus of World Poets Anthology", "Cadence", "AC Papa Literary Journal #3", and artwork alongside her ekphrastic poetry in "(a) River Rising Blooms", coming out this Fall. She is a member of the Ancient City Poets of St. Augustine, the National Federation of State Poetry Societies, and is President of the North Florida Poetry Hub, the local Chapter of the Florida State Poets Association in Jacksonville, Florida.

DEE WALLACE

Dee Wallace is an internationally known actress (250 films credits, six series, over 400 commercials) best known for her role as the mother in Steven Spielberg's *E.T.!* She has appeared on every major network and talk show, including *Oprah* and *The Today Show*, and has been featured on *E! True Hollywood Stories*. Ms. Wallace earned her teaching credentials from The University of Kansas, and has worked as a teacher in the public school system, as well as her own dance and acting studios. Ms. Wallace expanded her love of teaching, and the principles she found empowering for children, into daily sessions, a radio show and five books. Her work is based on the principles of accepting responsibility, and loving ourselves early in life to create the life we desire.

Dee is a strong advocate for accepting (at an early age) our own magnificence and power in a positive, loving way. A child's personality is set between 0-8 years of age which has a direct impact on the creation of their life. Dee's important message to the world is: Love yourself beyond anyone or anything else. Love yourself so much that you can't do anything that doesn't make you love yourself more.

Dee has authored five books on the subject of self-creation: *Conscious Creation, The Big E!, Bright Light, Getting Stuff* and *Wake Up Now!* She conducts a live (call-in) internet radio show each Sunday morning at 9 AM Pacific, and offers monthly webinars on a variety of creation subjects. Dee conducts private sessions from her home in Woodland Hills, California via phone and in person.

As a much sought after speaker, Dee has spoken at numerous national and international venues including the Love and Harmony Forum in Japan, The Dillon Lecture Series, Unity Temple, The Kansas Film Commission, and asked to speak in China, New Zealand, Amsterdam, Australia, England and all across the United States and Canada.

❧◊❧

TIM WATTS

Tim Watts is a former owner of an investment advisory firm. He and his wife, Edith Andersen, split their time between Fort Collins, Colorado and Ponte Vedra, Florida. They share love of family, reading, the outdoors, and insights gifted to them from caring people they meet.

Tim and Andrea Watts

ഉരു

SHEILA WEINSTEIN

Sheila Weinstein is a writer and pianist who grew up in New Jersey, was educated in New York City at Barnard College and obtained her MA degree in Music from Trinity University in San Antonio, Texas where her husband was head of the Division of Ophthalmology at the University of Texas Health Sciences Center. She taught piano privately there and when the family moved to West Virginia she began writing while continuing to teach piano at the Creative Arts Center of West Virginia University, and in her home. Their children grown and on their own, she and her husband moved to Florida where her husband opened a private practice. His practice ended when he was diagnosed with dementia. Several years later, when he entered a dementia facility, Sheila moved to New York City, alone for the first time in her life, having met her future husband when she was 16. There she decided to write about her journey and turned it into a book called *Moving to the Center of the Bed: The Artful Creation of a Life Alone*, which she hoped might help others. While writing the book, she took advantage of everything New York City had to offer, most especially becoming a docent at her beloved Carnegie Hall. In 2008 she was privileged to play her own compositions in Carnegie Hall's Weill Recital Hall. In 2014 she returned to Florida where she lives today. She has given courses at the Osher Lifelong Learning Institute on memoir writing, aging, and Carnegie Hall. She describes her docent work at Carnegie Hall as the most meaningful experience of her life. She is now 83 and writing a novel about Frederic Chopin.

BUZZ WILLIAMS

Buzz Williams graduated with multiple degrees in engineering plus an Executive MBA. After serving in the U.S. Coast Guard, he worked for more than 35 years in the construction industry in field supervision, sales, management, and corporate matters. He served on numerous Boards for the benefit of others. He aspires to be a loving, caring, generous, faithful father and husband who loves and works hard to demonstrate what a GOD-fearing person should be every day.